# STRESS MANAGEMENT

**Advance Praise for *Stress Management***

'I found myself recalling my own anxieties before a test and the fear of failure as I read the introduction to this book. I used to think no amount of studying or preparation would be sufficient and that the only solution would be postponing my exam. Perhaps if I had this book back then, I would have been better equipped to manage my anxieties. We all know how stress, when poorly managed, can negatively impact many aspects of our lives, including physical health, mental wellbeing, interpersonal relationships and occupational performance. *Stress Management* offers various straightforward strategies, including those from Hindu philosophy, to improve the management of stress in our lives. This book also addresses time management skills, the art of effective communication, the importance of forgiveness and gratitude, and other skill sets to better manage stressful circumstances. A particularly interesting concept for me was learning about gunas and how to manage them effectively in different circumstances. Regardless of our temperament, this book and its emphasis on stress management stands to enrich not just the quality of our lives but that of our loved ones as well.'

**—Adria C. Savino, MD, addiction psychiatrist**

'The author's description of active and default modes of the mind is supported by research in neuroscience, and it's surprisingly true that we tend to spend a significant portion of our time in the default mode, which can lead to distraction, stress and reduced focus. The comparison of the body and mind to a chariot, with intelligence as the charioteer and the soul as the passenger, is a common metaphor in Vedic wisdom and other spiritual traditions. It highlights the importance of controlling the mind and senses through the power of intelligence, to avoid being led astray by impulses and desires. When I read this book, I learnt invaluable lessons to manage my stress levels. As someone who has moved to the West from India, I appreciated the references to Vedic culture throughout the book.

'The author discusses the various sources of stress in our lives: stress caused by other living beings, stress caused by natural calamities and stress caused by internal factors like negative emotions and thought patterns. It offers advice on how to handle stress by controlling our minds and focusing on practical solutions. As someone who experiences stress daily, it was insightful to learn about the different types of stress and how to manage each one.'

**—Padmaja Puppala, MD, addiction psychiatrist**

'It is very interesting to learn about different phases of stress from the point of view of the East and how we can avoid the lower levels of stress altogether. It is fascinating to learn about the correlation between stress and impurities of the mind. I am very enlivened to learn about gunas and their impact on stress. By raising our consciousness, we can drastically reduce our stress. This is the new thing that I learnt, and it made a lot of sense to me. I encourage everyone to read and benefit from the knowledge shared in this book.'

**—Dan Fink, MD, occupational and environmental medicine physician**

# STRESS MANAGEMENT

A MONK'S WISDOM FOR PERSONAL FULFILLMENT AND PROFESSIONAL ACHIEVEMENT

**Yugal Kishore Das**

HARPER VANTAGE

HarperCollins *Publishers* India

First published in India in 2023 by Harper Vantage
An imprint of HarperCollins *Publishers*
4th Floor, Tower A, Building No. 10, DLF Cyber City,
DLF Phase II, Gurugram, Haryana – 122002
www.harpercollins.co.in

2 4 6 8 10 9 7 5 3 1



P-ISBN: 978-93-5699-736-3
E-ISBN: 978-93-5699-393-8



Typeset in 12/15.7 Palatino Linotype at
Manipal Technologies Limited, Manipal

Printed and bound at
Thomson Press (India) Ltd

FSC www.fsc.org MIX Paper from responsible sources FSC® C010615

This book is produced from independently certified FSC® paper to ensure responsible forest management.

*To my dear spiritual master,*
*H.H. Radhanath Swami*

# Contents

# Foreword

*The Art and Science of Self-Mastery* by my dear friend, Yugal Kishore Das, presents practical insights into stress, anger and time management. By combining powerful stories with life lessons, illustrations to reflect and remember, and questions at the end of each chapter to help you on a sincere journey towards self-mastery, Das offers a pragmatic guide to enhance your professional and personal lives. Grounded in the foundations of Vedic wisdom, Das comes up with a handy manual that allows us to look into our inner mirror. Covered by the dust of our imperfections—anger, greed, envy and pride—we are unable to see our reflections clearly in that mirror. Das offers valuable tools to clean this mirror so we can see ourselves clearly.

In the summer of 2022, I was approached by Dr Ramana Vinjamuri, our common friend and well-wisher, to write the foreword for this important contribution. Vinjamuri described the significance and the practical wisdom offered in these books for each and everyone of us. Inspired by our conversation, I quickly took to reading the manuscripts and could not put them down. Having been thus exhilarated, I found immense pleasure in writing this foreword.

I have known Yugal Kishore Das for more than twenty years. When I first met him, he was working as a software consultant with MetLife insurance company in Albany, New York. He would help arrange programmes for me in Albany. I would stay at his house during weekends. This programme eventually shaped into a university programme where we were preaching to the students at State University of New York, Albany. Many students were benefitted from this programme. This engagement made us good friends. He eventually received initiation from my spiritual master and became my spiritual brother and this brought us closer. He would regularly come to our monastery in Manhattan to understand the life of a monk. In that association, he felt that human life is meant for self-realization and this can be attained by selflessly serving humanity. This eventually led him to give up his job and join a monastery in West Virginia. I really appreciated his courage and sacrifice. He sacrificed his job and life for the benefit of others. Time and distance have not proved to be obstacles in our brotherhood. We regularly preached together on several occasions. He started extensively travelling and preaching the message all over America. It is for the benefit of the people that he writes these books.

There was once a retreat in Palace of Gold in West Virginia which I attended with other monks in our monastery. There was a discussion on the causes of various problems of the world. I remember Yugal Kishore Das saying that envy, anger and greed are the problems of mankind and by practising spirituality sincerely, one can eventually become free from these unwanted impurities of the heart. External problems are the outcome of internal problems. It was a lively discussion and other monks also shared their perspectives on the problems of the world. Why are oceans and rivers polluted? It is because every heart is polluted. Since the population is very large, this inner pollution would naturally reflect in rivers and oceans in a big way. So, ecological problems have a connection with the lack of spirituality in society and real spirituality must focus on cleansing the heart with an aim to leading a pure life. That way the world will become a better place to live in for everyone.

We met many times in this way and shared and expressed our opinions. Whenever we met, we would sit together and meditate for hours in the mornings. This has helped develop a camaraderie between us. I strongly feel this book will be beneficial to many as he has shared his valuable realizations and experiences.

There are three books in this series: *Stress Management, Anger Management* and *Time Management*. Each of these books is self-contained and written in an easy-to-understand manner with practical and eye-opening lessons embedded in each chapter. Each chapter ends with few questions that make you think and explore your inner self. The author has penned these parts and chapters in such a way that the reader can turn to any page and find something meaningful and pragmatic. By encouraging you to remember and recollect what you have read in the text, the illustrations help guide you further.

In *Time Management,* Yugal Kishore Das, emphasizing the importance of how time is precious, shares key principles of time management and why we need to manage our time, as well as the kind of obstacles that hinder us when we put these principles to practice. This is where we realize why we are unable to implement these familiar yet fruitful practices into our routines. The simplicity and clarity with which these tips are described will encourage each one of us to implement them in our daily lives and benefit from the author's wisdom.

In *Anger Management,* the author starts by describing the nuts and bolts of anger. The readers will be pleasantly surprised with insightful lessons where the author reveals how our anger shuts off our intelligence and acts against us. When we reach the peak of heightened anger in the spur of a moment, what we never think of are the consequences of our actions taken during those weak moments. If we are aware of these consequences, we would at least think before taking any action. The author takes a holistic approach on how we can prevent anger by understanding our inner self, our lifestyle and our thought process. Das closes this part with some sensible techniques on anger management. By presenting simple formulas and equations, he reveals our inner psyche. For example, the author talks about 7–38–55 rule in effective communication where it is not simply about our words. Only 7 per cent is the choice of words, 38 per cent is tone of voice and a majority, 55 per cent is our body language. Our body language and tone depend on our mood and mentality. The author guides us on nourishing and nurturing our inner self to groom our mood and mentality.

In *Stress Management*, Das begins with a touching story of his interaction with a student. Just with this one incident, I am confident that the readers can relate to and understand that stress is part of everyone's dictionary. He explains the fundamentals of stress and different stressors—knowledge derived from Vedic wisdom. He further talks about the lifecycle of stress. Awareness about these topics somehow brings a sense of calmness within us. Perhaps because we are able to understand that we are not the only ones stressed out and it gives out the hope that even if we are in the dark now, there will be light sooner than later. In the next chapters, Das gets into the details of the internal and external factors of stress and how these affect our body and mind. At this point, instead of stressing on stress, he takes us on an uplifting and optimistic journey on how we can avoid stress, and suggests some preventive measures using the principles of effective communication and anxiety management. Finally, he closes by presenting a practical skill set on how to manage stress. These are some of my favourite parts of the book as they present methods on how to practise forgiveness, gratitude and service. The readers are left at this point with key practices on relaxation, meditation and prayer.

In summary, I am confident that you will learn meaningful lessons in every page of this book just as I did. I encourage you to use these lessons, respond to the questions he poses at the end of each chapter, remember the tips and reflect on them, and, finally, adapt and apply them in your personal and professional lives.

As a techie, as a software engineer working for multinational companies, as a counsellor, as a life coach and as a monk in the West, Yugal Kishore Das had trekked a unique journey. From this unique journey comes his unique insights into the inner engineering that enables each one of us to turn our weaknesses such as anger, stress, sense of inferiority and procrastination into our strengths such as inner peace, composure, determination and confidence.

**Pandit Dasa**
mindful leadership expert and
motivational speaker,
*USA Today*'s 'Top 8 Influential Speakers to
Follow' in 2002,
author of bestsellers *Urban Monk* and
*Closing the Apps*
For more information, please
visit: www.panditdasa.com

# Preface

Usually, it is medical doctors and research scientists who write books on such topics. So, what made me (a monk) write these books?

As technology started developing with a singular motive to make our lives better, paradoxically and interestingly, our lives started becoming more and more mechanical. Despite technology being at its peak today, we all have become very disoriented in our lives. In the US alone, an astounding number of people have mental health problems. We live in the time of a lot of social unrest.

Why is there so much social unrest globally? It is because everyone is experiencing a lot of internal unrest, one within themselves. Why is there this unrest at an individual and internal level? When we face disturbance on a physical, mental or emotional level, it disturbs or inner peace. Apart from this, nature too offers us challenges in the form of extreme weather, cyclones, floods, earthquakes and tsunamis, etc. In this world where everyone is quarrelling with each other, there is always somebody or something that seems to disturb our peace. Mental and physical ailments also cause us a lot of stress. Apart from this, the world of today is becoming increasingly global. Hence, a slight disturbance caused in one part of the world spirals out to affect people in the other part of the world, making them frustrated and depressed. Stress, anxiety, frustration and depression have become the buzz words in this busy world.

Managing our stress, anger and time on a daily basis has become especially difficult. Everyone seems to be extremely busy. But by the end of the hectic day, they realize that they have truly accomplished only a little. This makes them unhappy.

Stress is a common problem in society. We all have a list of things to address. Some demand our immediate attention. But we may not have enough resources to manage these tasks or to deal with the resultant stress.

When we are busy addressing and sorting out everyday problems all the time, our body finds itself constantly in the fight-and-flight mode, with very little rest. In such a state, things are bound to go wrong, and, as a result, we also become angry.

How do we make ourselves immune to all these problems? That is the subject matter of these books. For example, we must understand that we have no control over tomorrow's weather or how our boss is going to act with us, but we have control over how *we* react. By developing the right mindset and/or by taking precautionary measures, we can either minimize the problem or totally avoid the problem. For example, if the tree is healthy and strong and firmly rooted deep within the soil, it can weather any type of storms or overcome threats posed by any type of pests. In the same way, if we can become strong and firm, we can face the storms of life. What are the tools we need to make us firmly rooted within ourselves to face any type of disturbance or adversity in our lives?

I write these books to equip people with the necessary tools needed to deal with the common problems of life that we all face on a day-to-day basis. First step in that direction is awareness and acceptance of the problems, and recognizing the need to address them. Of course, for that to happen, we need to have a very good understanding of our mind and sense organs, and their collective functioning in both relaxed as well as problematic environments.

Since the mind, as opposed to the brain, is not a physical organ but a very intangible one, its behaviour is unpredictable and differs from individual to individual. Once, I was conducting a seminar in a college on the positive attitude of the mind. After the seminar, a student came to me and said, 'If only you had come two weeks ago and conducted this seminar, my friend would not have committed suicide.' Moved, I asked him why he felt like that. He said, the presentation was mentally very uplifting and gave so much hope and strength to deal with the problems of life.

During my research, I was fascinated to find how our mind operates differently at different times and different environments. It is very interesting to note that our mind picks up all of the information that we gullibly and inadvertently collect through our various experiences. But when we want to erase it from our mind, it is not easy to erase them. These thoughts circulate in our minds for a very long time. I tried to find the relation between the nature around us, our impulsive thoughts and the reactions of the body to them. The reality is our senses constantly demand enjoyment. But our mind being connected to our senses has the ability control them. However, the mind is fickle and gets distracted easily, without bothering about the consequences. This is a serious problem, and many people are not aware of this problem. Intelligence is superior to the mind and hence can control the senses. If we can sharpen our intelligence and control the mind, our life becomes much better. In fact, learning this truth led me to take up the meditation process more seriously, whereby I tried to restrain the demands of the mind and the senses with a sharpened intelligence.

I have been meditating for more than twenty-five years on a daily basis. I am myself fascinated with the results. I was part of Henry Ford Hospital research team which conducted research on the efficacy of mantra meditation (where you meditate by chanting on a mantra) and its effect on the brain. Based on my experience in dealing with the mind, I have developed a few tools and a lifestyle whereby one can handle anxiety and stress. With these tools, I have been counselling hundreds of professionals from the corporate world, as well as many families and students for more than twenty-one years in the US and other countries, and have helped them cope with stress, anxiety, anger and depression.

My training is based on imparting knowledge on the internal aspects of our physical bodies—their functioning and their inter-relationships.

I provide separate tools to handle the physical body, the internal space of the mind and the deeper intellect. When we realize that we, as consciousness, are different from our physical organs and that it is our thoughts that lead us to action, we become careful with our thought process. This is where we need help and training. With proper guidance and practice, we can alter various negative patterns of our mind to positive patterns, and bring a revolutionary change in our actions and in our lives.

I have mentioned many examples and case studies in these books for the benefit of the reader. If you are able to get some benefit out of them, I will be most happy as a monk and consider this little endeavour fruitful.

Your humble servant,<br>
Yugal Kishore Das<br>
Michigan (USA), 17 July 2023

# Introduction

One day, while I was absorbed in meditation, my phone rang. My initial reaction was to ignore the call and make a mental note to return it later, as I try to block off time in the morning for my spiritual upliftment. But when the phone began ringing again, I realized there could be an emergency that needed my immediate attention and rose to answer the phone. It was John, a brilliant student preparing for his MCAT, a necessary step in his mission to become a successful doctor in the US. I asked him what I could do for him.

Suddenly, he broke into tears. 'I can't do it. I cannot take this exam! I will fail! Everyone will laugh at me! My parents will lose all trust in me! I am good for nothing!'

'But you have been preparing well for months, haven't you?' I asked reassuringly.

'My preparation has been very bad. I've just been pretending all these months. I can't do it!' he replied.

'You were very confident last week. What happened today?'

'No, no, it was all superficial. I'm not adequately prepared. I can't do it. It would be better for me to not even take it.'

There was no confidence in his voice. He was morose. Above all, he was stressed out. He was going through test anxiety, a very common experience amongst students. I had known him for a few years and knew he was both intelligent and hard-working.

Test anxiety is a type of performance anxiety. Students, athletes and performers often experience it. The Yerkes–Dodson law suggests that performance increases with mental arousal only up to a certain point. After that point, performance tends to decrease.

I said, 'I still encourage you to take the exam in order to gain experience. You will get a better idea of your preparedness. Even if you don't get a good score this time, you'll be more prepared next time.'

'No. Everything has evaporated from my brain. I don't remember anything.' Finally, he emphatically declared, 'I am *not* going to take the exam.'

'We can come to a well-reasoned decision together,' I replied. 'You still have three weeks to decide. With your preparation, I feel you will do well and get into a good medical school. You are truly a bright student. You can take the exam and wait for the result. Your score will not be the end of the world. For now, get some rest. We will discuss this again tomorrow.'

Leading up to the exam, he would call me every day and I would counsel and encourage him. I would try to convince him that he was a brilliant student, that he would surely get a good score and that there was no loss in trying. I assured him that his parents were always there to support him and love him irrespective of the outcome of this test. I related to him the premise of the Bhagavad Gita. The soldier Arjuna, faced with having to decide whether to fight or not, found himself confused, insecure and paranoid. Krishna then explained to him the art of performing one's duty without being attached to the results. Slowly, our doctor-to-be had a change of heart. He decided to take the test, although deep down, the fear remained.

Gradually, as days went by, he regained his confidence. On the day of the exam, he promised me that he would simply try his best and not worry about the result. After that, we eagerly awaited his score. I am very happy to report that he indeed received an exceptional score and got into the medical school of his choice.

It's very easy to succumb to pressure and end up far from the realization of one's full potential, but, equipped with the proper understanding, one can rise above stressful conditions and succeed.

***

If we are well-prepared to face a challenge, we won't be as stressed as we otherwise would have been; we will be stimulated just enough to be fully effective. This little amount of stress is called positive stress and it helps get us focused and ready to perform. If we are so stressed out that we panic, that stress overwhelms our mental faculties and takes away from our performance. This force is so powerful that it can inhibit even our ability to do basic things that we are normally able to do with ease.

Stress is a widespread, debilitating disease. The World Health Organization declared stress to be the health epidemic of the century.[1] Although this century has ushered us into a digital revolution, there's no escaping the fact that the quality of consciousness has degraded and people are becoming more and more stressed out.

The effect stress has on mankind is huge. In 2019, an article by the American Institute of Stress presented the following startling statistics: 83 per cent of US workers suffer from work-related stress; US businesses lose up to $300 billion yearly as a result of workplace stress; stress causes around one million workers to miss work every day; only 43 per cent of US employees think their employers care about their work–life balance; depression leads to $51 billion in costs due to absenteeism and $26 billion in treatment costs; work-related stress causes 1,20,000 deaths and results in $190 billion in healthcare costs yearly.

Consider also the following facts, published by the Global Organization for Stress:

1 George Fink, 'Stress: The Health Epidemic of the 21st Century', Scitechconnect.esvier.com, 26 April 2016, https://scitechconnect.elsevier.com/stress-health-epidemic-21st-century/#:~:text=%E2%80%9CStress%E2%80%9D%20has%20been%20dubbed%20the,physical%20health%20can%20be%20devastating

- 75 per cent of adults reported experiencing moderate to high levels of stress in the past month and nearly half reported that their stress has increased in the past year.—*American Psychological Association (September, 2022)*
- Approximately one out of seventy-five people experience a panic disorder.—*National Institute of Mental Health*
- Stress is a top health concern for US teens between the ninth and twelfth grades. Psychologists say that if they do not learn how to manage that stress in healthy ways, it could have serious long-term health implications. —*American Psychological Association*
- 80 per cent of workers feel stress on the job and nearly half say they need help in learning how to manage stress. 42 per cent say their co-workers need such help.—*American Institute of Stress*
- Stress levels in the workplace are rising, with six out of every ten workers in major global economies experiencing increased workplace stress.—*The Regus Group*
- Alarmingly, 91 per cent of Australians adults feel stressed about at least one important

aspect of their lives. Almost 50 per cent feel very stressed about one aspect of life.—*Lifeline Australia*

- Australian employees are absent for an average of 3.2 working days each year due to stress. This workplace stress costs the Australian economy approximately A$14.2 billion per year.—*Medibank*

Now, let's take a deeper look at this all-pervasive ailment and determine how we can manage it before it consumes us.

# CHAPTER 1

# What Is Stress?

Stress is the body's natural response when faced with a challenging situation. The American Institute of Stress defines it as 'physical, mental, or emotional strain or tension' or 'a condition or feeling experienced when a person perceives that demands exceed the personal and social resources the individual is able to mobilize'.

In the 1930s, Hans Selye, also called the 'Father of Stress', an endocrinologist at McGill University, demonstrated with his experiments that, irrespective of the circumstances producing the stress, the response and reaction of the body is the same.[2] The changes the body goes through

2 Siang Yong Tan and A. Yip, 'Hans Selye (1907–1982): Founder of the stress theory', *Singapore Medical Journal*, Vol. 59 No. 4 (April, 2018), https://www.ncbi.nlm.nih.gov/pmc/articles/PMC5915631/

prepare the body to aptly deal with the distressing situation. In this sense, stress can help us solve the various issues we're faced with. This is positive stress. However, a body under prolonged exposure to stress generates excessive quantities of hormones and chemicals, which leads to disease.

To understand how stress affects us, let us learn about how the body functions.

## 1.1. THE BRAIN, THE MIND, THE YOGA OF BODY AND SOUL

Our body is an amazing machine. It is thousands of times more complex than even the most high-tech car. If we analyse the human body, we will surely appreciate the intelligence behind its design. Everything in the world is drawn downwards due to gravity, yet our blood flows upwards, towards the brain, at all times. Our eyes are the clearest of cameras, our voice box the perfect musical instrument, our heart an almost inexhaustible engine that pumps blood for decades on end.

In a computer, we observe different forms of hardware and software. We can compare our physical body to the hardware of a computer, our mind to its software which makes the body function, and our soul to the user. The soul works with the hardware (body) and the software (mind) to pursue its goals. For one to effectively use the computer, the hardware and software must function properly. According to Vedic wisdom, we are neither this body (hardware) nor this mind (software): we are the soul, the user of the body and mind.

Psychiatrists agree that our mind functions in two modes: an active mode and a default mode. When our mind is in the active mode, it actively thinks, feels and wills, based on a given set of stimuli. In contrast, in default mode, it simply wanders aimlessly, journeying sometimes into the past and dwelling on past experiences and at other times into the future to worry about what's to come. We spend at least 50 per cent of life in this default mode.

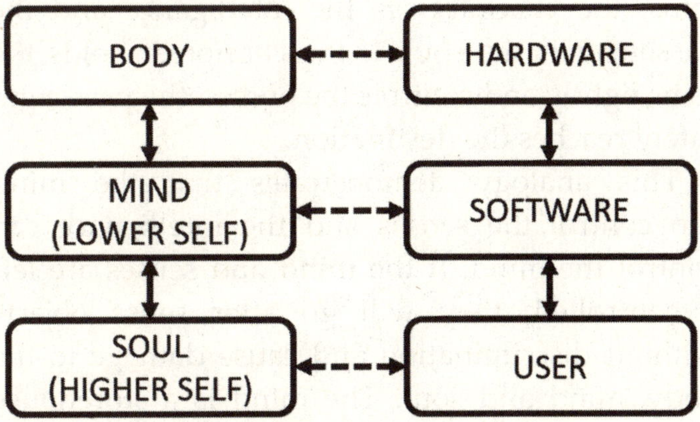

At any point in time, there are numerous different thought processes active in our brain, and we tend to jump from one process to another aimlessly. This drains our mental energy. Just as having many apps open on a phone drains its battery, the wandering mind lost in various aimless trains of thought loses its ability to focus. Such an untamed mind is liable to cause us a lot of stress.

## The Chariot Model

Vedic wisdom provides us with the beautiful analogy of a chariot to help us understand the connection between the body, mind and soul. According to this comparison, our body is a chariot. Our five senses (eyes, nose, ears, tongue and skin) are five wild horses. They always look for sense objects. Our mind is represented by the reins, the charioteer is the intelligence and the passenger is the soul. If the charioteer holds the reins tightly and controls the horses, the passenger safely reaches the destination.

This analogy demonstrates that the mind can control the senses and the intelligence can control the mind. If the mind and senses are left uncontrolled, they will go after sense objects without discrimination and cause damage to the body, mind and soul. The mind is a storehouse of our past experiences. By nature, the mind is very impulsive. Like a computer that processes everything in terms of binary logic, the mind tends to say either yes or no immediately. In order to make a decision, the mind asks only one question: 'Is it painful or pleasurable?' If it is painful, the mind will reject it; if pleasurable, it will be accepted. But the mind does not evaluate the repercussions of its decisions. Thus, we often find ourselves regretting decisions made simply based on pleasure or pain.

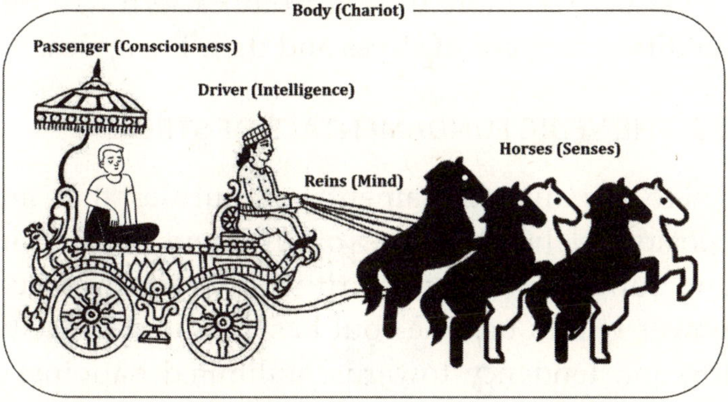


Intelligence is the discerning factor. Intelligence evaluates the outcome of a decision and provides the reasoning for it. If our intelligence is sharp enough to control our mind, we can avoid many pitfalls. The same problem or situation can generate positive stress in someone and negative stress in someone else. Intelligence is the primary difference between someone who is energized with positive stress and someone who is debilitated by negative stress.

On very hot, sunny days, when small plants die due to heat, big trees thrive. In the same way, those who have sharper intelligence can control their minds on stressful days. The solution to stress management lies in cultivating intelligence that can handle the mind. This will be discussed in later chapters.

Let us gain more insight from Eastern wisdom on different types of stress and their life cycles.

## 1.2. THE VEDIC FUNDAMENTALS OF STRESS

There are five fundamental impurities that are considered the root causes of stress and lead to pain and suffering. We are spirit souls with unlimited power within us. The soul has a natural capacity for, and tendency towards, unlimited happiness, knowledge and bliss. When we are forgetful of this fact, due to ignorance, we become absorbed in bodily consciousness. The internal impurities that lead us to experience stress and anxiety are avidya (ignorance), asmita (false ego), raga (attachment to temporary things), dvesha (aversion) and abhinivesha (absorption in bodily consciousness).

Let's take a closer look at these roots now so that we can perfectly deal with and most probably eliminate negative stress altogether.

### Avidya (Ignorance)

Due to ignorance, we think we are our body. Vedic wisdom emphasizes that we are not our physical external bodies but spirit souls within the bodies. As has been mentioned, the soul is the driver of the chariot of the body and the senses are like horses that will pull the chariot in different directions unless the charioteer (intelligence) grasps the reins tightly and relies on values other than the pursuit of pleasure to guide the chariot towards destinations where one can find genuine happiness and fulfilment. We should align our goals with our ultimate happiness. To instead base them on short-term pleasures yields only wild discontent and stress. True happiness and, indeed, true success come from discipline employed for a higher cause, a deeper cause, one that starts within.

The characteristics of the body are quite the opposite of those of the soul. The physical body is temporary and gives us more pain than pleasure. Vedic wisdom teaches us that, due to avidya or ignorance, we misidentify with the temporary body and subtle mind. This misidentification

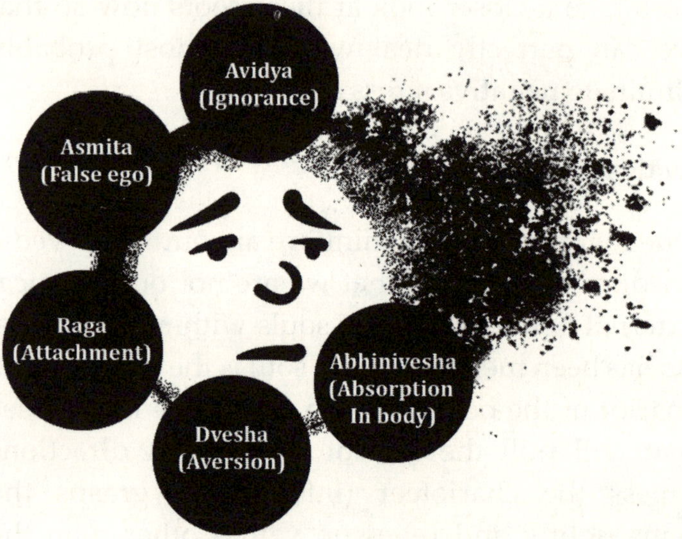


makes us very passionate about actions that lead to quick results and temporary sensual enjoyment. Forgetting that happiness actually resides deep within us, our senses try to derive happiness through sense objects. The tongue tries to find happiness by tasting different foods, the eyes by seeing beautiful things, the nose by smelling fragrant aromas, the ear by listening to melodious music, the skin through pleasurable contact. Other species also do the same things to derive pleasure. However, these kinds of pleasures are short-lived and often give way to various forms of stress in time.

### Asmita (False Ego)

Vedic wisdom highlights that our true identity is to be anchored in an eternal soul that is full of knowledge and bliss. We tend to forget this when we start identifying with the temporary material body. Impelled by our false ego, we identify ourselves with the temporary designations of this world—'I am a doctor'; 'I am an engineer'; 'I am an American'; 'I am a businessman'; 'I am a father'; 'I am a mother', etc. We then build a false sense of ownership around these roles. When there is a threat to this control we've mentally assumed, we try to defend our position. Amidst these power struggles lies a great deal of stress.

### Raga (Attachment)

Eastern philosophy teaches us that the nature of the soul is to be happy. Problems arise when we forget our spiritual nature and identify with the temporary body. Since the nature of the soul is to be happy, we try to find happiness through various sensual pleasures and then develop attachment to temporary objects connected to the body. We build relationships in connection with the body, acquire sense objects for our enjoyment, develop attachments to those objects that give us pleasure and thus grow more and more entangled in attempts to find happiness. Our body, spouse, children, home, job, bank balance, relatives, friends, social status and prestige are a few of our common attachments. When these attachments are harmed or likely to be harmed, we become stressed out.

### Dvesha (Aversion)

Vedic philosophy defines dvesha or aversion as a negative emotional reaction towards unpleasant objects, people or circumstances. Our negative reactions are based on our previous experiences. When we are overcome by aversion, we cannot bear the presence of individuals (e.g., running into a former manager you had conflicts with), situations (e.g., travelling through places of trauma) or objects (e.g., photos or souvenirs of individuals who have left bitter memories in your life) associated with those experiences. When we are presented with these unpleasant situations, we experience various kinds of stress.

### Abhinivesha (Absorption in Bodily Consciousness)

Vedic philosophy explains that our absorption in bodily consciousness makes us forget that we are eternal by nature; due to this, we develop a fear of death. When we are absorbed in bodily consciousness, we are forced by our conditioning to always think of everything in terms of the body. This results in fear. We develop a fear of losing the objects to which we are attached and a fear of encountering those objects we are averse to. We fear losing our bodies; after all, death is nothing but loss of the body. Vedic wisdom reiterates that, as souls, we continue to live eternally. For those who have a control over their mind and senses, death is but a paper tiger. But, when we forget that we are spirit souls and become absorbed instead in bodily consciousness, fear arises. This fear can lead to severe levels of stress. When we experience a death in the family or of a friend or ourselves undergo a severe terminal illness, we then experience severe stress.

Now let us look at the different states in the life cycle of stress.

## 1.3. THE STRESS CYCLE

Understanding the progression of stress from the subtle to the gross state renders us better able to deal with it when it begins to appear. There are four cycles of stress, according to the ancient yoga sutras: prasupta (dormant state), tanu (weakened state), vicchinna (absent state) and udaram (active state).

### Prasupta (Dormant State)

Our attitudes, initiatives, relationships and actions can initiate dormant stress. Dormant stress is likened to a seed in the ground. When we sow a seed in the ground, it is not visible on the surface immediately. But it is there. When the right conditions appear, it will sprout and eventually produce fruits. In the same way, dormant stress eventually manifests in gross ways that end up creating more distressing situations. By identifying stress seeds and taking proper action, we can convert dormant stress into positive emotions or, at the very least, kill the stress tree before it sprouts.

For example, let us consider an envious person. When they see someone performing at a higher level than they are performing at, they start disliking the person. As the other person gets better and better results, the envious person's heart boils over with envy. These feelings generate a lot of stress. Here, the problem is not the successful person but the impure heart of the envious one. An impure heart is a fertile garden for stress. When one hears of the superior qualities of another, the seed of stress is sown. By identifying this seed and actively finding ways to appreciate the person instead of looking for their faults, one can prevent its germination. Remember to take the steps necessary to disable these dormant stressors before they take root.

One of the major characters in the Mahabharata was a famous prince named Duryodhana, who was envious by nature. He was also very arrogant. His five cousins, collectively called the Pandavas, were very talented and this caused his envy to steadily build. Once, during a famous event, observing how deeply the various kings respected the Pandavas and how they honoured them with gifts and kind words, Duryodhana became inflamed with envy. This envy caused him to sow the seed of perpetual stress in his heart. As the Pandavas became more successful, this seed grew into a big tree that produced more fruits of stress and anxiety for Duryodhana. If he had addressed his envy and worked *with* the Pandavas instead of praying for their downfall, he would have grown enormously, both internally and materially. Instead, his envious and arrogant nature became a rock-hard barrier in his life and brought him untold anxiety, depression and, eventually, destruction.

Another example is of a person with a controlling nature. He loves and thoroughly enjoys his position as a manager of a company. As the head of his family, he enjoys controlling his dependents. He always wants things to happen *his* way. He wants everyone to listen to and obey him. When any family member does something without informing him, his ego gets hurt. This quality sows the seed of stress, as no one wants to be controlled by others. In this example, the controlling mentality is the cause of the stress. At work, when this person sees someone producing better and better results, he becomes insecure, fearing that this successful someone might replace him in the near future. As other team members improve their performances, his internal stress increases and eventually turns into anxiety. The seed of the stress is his attachment to his position and his controlling mentality.

In ancient Indian texts, King Indra, the ruler of the heavenly planets, is described as very attached to heavenly pleasures. Whenever he would notice someone performing austerities and penances, he would assume that they were trying to claim his throne. This would disturb him and provoke him to send celestial damsels to disturb the person he had developed suspicions against. Lack of success in such endeavours would cause Indra to become very stressed out. The stressor or seed of stress here is his attachment to his position and to enjoying heavenly pleasures.

In summary envy, ego, a controlling nature, attachment and the intense desire to enjoy earthly pleasures are the root causes of stress.

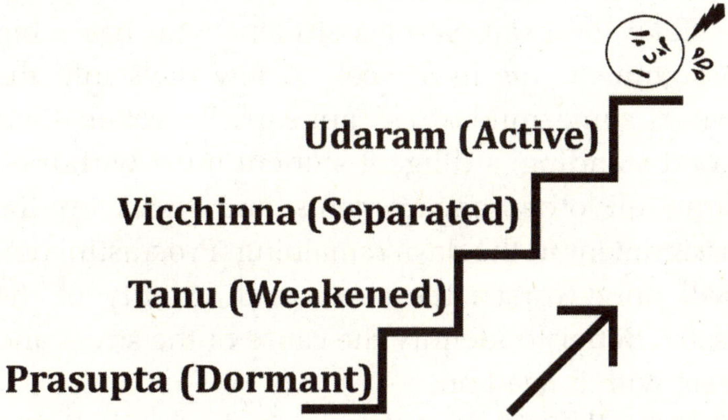


### Tanu (Weakened State)

In this next stage of stress, the seed of stress has already sprouted. The effects are visible. This is the stage in which the distressing situation has come to a head and the only two options are to take action to deal with it promptly or to procrastinate and prolong the disturbance. If the situation demands a change of attitude, we must be ready to adapt. If we need to allocate more time to a task, we must do so. If we feel we don't have enough resources to handle the situation, we must allocate more resources at this stage. If it seems the challenge is no longer worth our time and resources, we can also choose to withdraw at this stage. Overall, this means that there is a problem on our hands, but we still have time to subdue it.

Take the example of a student who has a big assignment due in a week. A few days into the week, some mild stress appears. To retain their good standing, a diligent student must withdraw from all other engagements and focus on the assignment in the days remaining. Procrastination will only worsen the stress and severity of the issue. Better to identify the cause of the stress and deal with it head on.

Overall, this is still an initial stage, one in which we experience stress without being wholly consumed by it. This is the stage at which we must take the proper steps to turn the tide in our favour. We must pay attention, as the enemy has surfaced. We have the opportunity to respond positively, fight it out and gain more self-assurance. The time has come to address the challenge. Respond before it is too late.

### Vicchinna (Separated State)

In this subtler state, the stressor is in our psyche but in a subconscious state. For various reasons, the stressor has not strongly manifested at the forefront of our mind. We might be deliberately avoiding it, physically distant from the cause or just fully occupied with other things. A certain environment, person or event may cause this subconscious stress to more grossly manifest. For example, when you visit a place where you've suffered in the past, you might ruminate on the experiences you had there. Other examples are meeting with a divorced spouse or getting back into a car after a bad accident. Students conducting research at any university usually meet their professor on a weekly basis to report their progress; if, for some reason, the professor is away for a month and the student doesn't have any remarkable progress to report, the thought of the upcoming meeting will cause stress. But since the meeting is not scheduled to happen yet, the student is separated from the stressful state. These examples demonstrate that, in this stage, the stressor is present in the psyche but only manifests under certain conditions.

### Udaram (Active State)

In this state, the stressor is fully active. We may experience an imbalance in our life as a result. The stressor resides at the forefront of our mind. Despite our best attempts, we find that we don't have enough resources to handle the situation, which causes lot of stress. These stressors may arise as a result of our ego, attachments, aversions or our absorption in bodily consciousness. Imagine having to give a presentation to your most valuable customers in the presence of your boss to clinch a contract, but being totally unprepared—this would cause stress in an active state. You appear for a job interview with very little or no preparation—this would cause lot of stress. You have been fighting your ill health for a long time but there is no sign of recovery—this would cause stress to be in the active state. You have an important meeting to get to but you find out that your flight has been delayed to the extent that everything will need to progress perfectly from that point onwards for you to be able to make it to the meeting at a reasonable time. You and your partner are engaged in an argument and both of you feel stressed about your respective opinions not being heard. There are many other obvious forms of active stress. Can you think of any that appear in your life?

### 1.4. DIFFERENT TYPES OF STRESSORS

Eastern wisdom texts identify several stressors. These stressors comprehensively cover the different types of fear that we all experience—fears and stresses caused by disease, progeny, money, dishonour, competition, enemies, old age and, finally, death. Let's discuss each one of them so as to better understand the kinds of hurdles we may face.

### Physical Ailments

Many people shudder at the thought of physical setbacks. While inconvenient, these diseases or accidents can also trigger a kind of stress that motivates us to fight against their effects. America's first big-screen Superman, Christopher Reeve, was a good example of this. When he met with an accident while riding a horse, he became paralysed from the neck down for the rest of his life. Instead of just lamenting his physical circumstances, he used his remaining time to be an inspiration to other handicapped people. Accidents are bound to happen; the important thing is how we respond to them. After his accident, Reeve lived for eight more years, travelling and helping others overcome their setbacks until his last day.

Actually, the body is bound to be incapacitated at one point or another. But because, as we discussed, we are different from the body—eternal spirit souls—we never need to give up. There is never any question of the incapacitation or death of the soul. If we understand this fact, we can accept the changes in our life with courage and determination.

One day, I received a phone call from a woman named Mary. She was happily raising her two young children until she was suddenly diagnosed with breast cancer. She and her husband then became very depressed. She had to juggle her ravaging disease, the side effects of chemotherapy, tending to her children and a seemingly insurmountable amount of mental stress. It was very painful to watch. I would regularly counsel her and try to inspire her. Her friends in the community also offered her support and moral strength. Every day, we not only offered prayers for her recovery but remained present with her through her painful journey. Not the type to easily give up, she fought the disease with the help of her husband and friends and is now almost fully recovered.

We can gain wisdom from the pages of the Gita that tell us we are not the body but a powerful spirit soul. In fact, this is one of the first lessons of spirituality. The Gita says that the body is an external dress covering the soul. The way our clothes get worn down, this body eventually wanes, picks up diseases and finally dies. This happens to everyone. However, there is no death for the spirit soul. If we understand this fact, we can accept the changes in our life with courage.

## Progeny

Children play a very important role in society. Some people are stressed out because they don't have any children. Some are stressed out because their children do not listen to them. Others are worried that their children are falling behind in school. The list goes on and on.

The Bhagavat Purana tells the story of King Chitraketu, who had almost everything one could ever hope for in this world: wealth, position, unlimited power and all the things that came with his throne. Yet, he was depressed because he had no children. Eventually, one of his queens gave birth to a baby boy. The king was elated! However, just a short time later, his only child died, leaving King Chitraketu in an ocean of grief. The king was so depressed that he nearly died. However, with the counsel of monks who imparted spiritual guidance to him, he recovered.

## Money

Money is as sweet as honey to many. However, our desires and often even our needs can tend to exceed our financial resources. Thus, stress ensues. 25 per cent of Americans worry about their money either most or all of the time. More than 50 per cent of

Americans worry about medical bills, 54 per cent worry about retirement, 36 per cent about college expenses, 36 per cent about monthly expenses and 30 per cent about rent and mortgage.

There are a few ways to alleviate financial fears:

1. Create a separate savings account and cultivate the habit of saving on a regular basis. This will come to your rescue during emergencies.
2. Steady income obviates financial insecurity. Try to acquire assets from where you receive extra income on a regular basis.
3. Adjust your lifestyle according to your income and avoid unnecessary spending; this will save you from financial woes and financial stress.
4. We should try to lead a debt-free life to the greatest possible extent. If you do not have debts, you are financially safe. Plus, a debt-free life boosts one's confidence.
5. Rather than showing others how happy you are by buying luxurious things, lead a life that will truly make YOU happy. To experience inner joy, practice meditation and prayer.

6. Plan for the future and have a retirement account dedicated to future financial stability.

Timely guidance and the support of a financial counsellor will bring you out of your financial woes. Discussing your financial situation with a dear family member and/or a friend and seeking their advice may help. If it leads to anxiety and sleeplessness and the situation is beyond control, seek medical assistance.

## Dishonour

The Bhagavad Gita says that, to a respectable person, dishonour is worse than death. While not always so crippling, dishonour is always very painful. Memories of humiliation haunt us for a very long time. Consider the example of Emperor Valerian.[3] Roman emperors commanded a lot of respect during their reign and wielded much power. Valerian was one such emperor. As soon as he assumed the position, he had to face many internal and external challenges. He received a threat from the Sassanian emperor, Shahpur. Valerian led his armies to the battle of Edessa to defeat his enemy's

3 Valerian (emperor), Wikipedia, https://en.wikipedia.org/wiki/Valerian_(emperor)

forces. Surprisingly, Valerian was defeated in the battle and captured as a prisoner of war. As a prisoner, he was often humiliated. King Shahpur used him as a footstool. Enemy soldiers would abuse him with scornful words. Unable to endure the mortification, Valerian died in 260 CE.

### Competition

In any workplace, classroom or sports field, when we come across an opponent, we start to feel uneasy. All types of competitors face stress. In individual sports like tennis, the stress is even more prominent.

The battle between Thomas Edison and Nikola Tesla in the 1880s is famously referred to as the War of the Currents.[4] Edison developed the direct current (DC) that ran in a single direction, as is the case with batteries. The problem with DC is that it is not easy to alter its voltage. Tesla felt that an alternating current (AC) would solve the problem. AC could reverse its direction a few times a second. Employing a transformer would also allow for the current to easily be converted into different voltages. Edison, who was earning royalties on

4 'The War of the Currents: AC vs. DC Power', Energy.gov, 18 November 2014, https://www.energy.gov/articles/war-currents-ac-vs-dc-power

his DC patents, publicly rejected the usage of AC and its advantages and started a campaign to malign AC. However, when the whole of Buffalo, New York, was lit up using AC, the reality of AC's supremacy began to set in. Eventually, the whole world came to embrace the advantages of AC.

### Enemies

Any person, whether weak or powerful, must worry about opponents. Elephants are some of the most powerful animals to roam the jungles, but they are terrified of lions. Male lions especially pose a great threat to them, and elephants are well aware of this fact. Karen McComb of the University of Sussex found that, when elephants hear a recording of a lion's roar, they become stressed and immediately usher their herd into a defensive formation. The same goes for politics and business; people involved in these fields must be ever vigilant against the advances of the opposition and are constantly acting to fortify their positions. This causes a lot of stress.

### Wickedness

The virtuous fear the wicked. When wicked people try to vilify the virtuous and tarnish their reputation, it causes stress to the latter. There is a story in the Srimad Bhagavat Purana about King Kamsa that is relevant in this context. When the king heard a prophecy that foretold of his death by the eighth child of his sister, he became outraged and imprisoned his sister Devaki and her husband Vasudeva. The two had to deal with extreme stress due to this, despite being free from faults.

### Ageing

When we're young, it can be hard to imagine that we will one day grow old. Once we start to observe wrinkles on our face, we tend to become a bit stressed. In today's culture, everyone identifies ageing with losing charm, beauty and opportunities. Stress thus naturally ensues as one feels their youthful qualities wearing thin.

### Death

People fear death. Many people don't even want to talk about the idea of dying. When someone dear to us dies, we become depressed. When someone is nearing death, they become very terrified. We develop attachments to people, then death painfully cuts those connections. Death can be one of the most distressing circumstances any human being experiences.

In some of his lesser-known work, Sir Isaac Newton conducted experiments with the hope of making people immortal. He worked on finding an alchemical recipe for the philosopher's stone. Walt Disney was interested in cryogenics, hoping that the field would eventually achieve a breakthrough in making human immortality possible. There are many affluent people who are working towards this goal, as death brings everything to an end. A California billionaire has long been working with anti-ageing technologies. He has invested in companies dedicated to increasing the human lifespan, with the ultimate goal of cracking the code of immortality. Only time will tell whether all these efforts will culminate in success!

## SUMMARY

### Fundamentals of Stress

Definition: A condition or feeling experienced when someone perceives that demands exceed the personal and social resources they can mobilize.

Body: Hardware
Mind: Software
Soul: User

Root causes of stress according to Vedic texts:

- Ignorance
- False ego
- Attachment
- Aversion
- Absorption in bodily consciousness

Life cycle of stress:

- Dormant state
- Weakened state
- Separated state
- Active state

Different types of stressors:

- Physical ailments
- Progeny
- Money
- Dishonour
- Enemies
- Competition
- Ageing
- Death

### QUESTIONS

1. What do you think is the root cause of stress?

____________________

____________________

____________________

____________________

2. When was the last time you experienced stress or anxiety? Which one of the stressors was the cause?

___

___

___

___

3. What should you do when you realize that your stress is in a dormant state?

___

___

___

___

4. What should you do when you realize that your stress is in a weakened state?

___

___

___

___

5. You are regularly stuck in traffic jams on your way to the office in the morning, which causes you stress. What are the different solutions you can apply to avoid stress in this situation?

______________________________________

______________________________________

______________________________________

______________________________________

6. A prolonged physical ailment is causing you stress. What should you do?

______________________________________

______________________________________

______________________________________

______________________________________

# CHAPTER 2

# Identifying the Roots

## 2.1. EXTERNAL FACTORS

Now we will consider the different internal and external factors that stress us out. The external factors are divided into two categories: stress caused by other living beings (adhibhautika) and stress caused by environmental or natural calamities (adhidaivika).

### Stress Caused by Other Living Beings

There will always be someone who gives us trouble. For some people, it is their boss; for others, it is either a friend, a family member or a neighbour. Stress at the workplace is common these days. According to the American Institute of Stress, the main causes of workplace stress are workload (39 per cent of workers), interpersonal issues (31 per cent), juggling work and personal life (19 per cent) and job security (6 per cent).

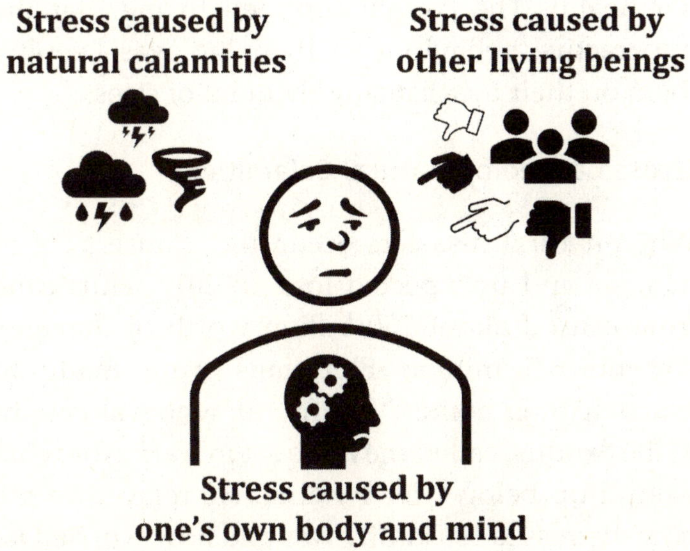


Relationship issues are some of the major examples of situational stressors. In the early 19th century, divorce was uncommon in the United States. Today, nearly 50 per cent of marriages end in divorce. There are many causes for divorce, but the effects are always stressful no matter what. For some parents, children are the problem, and for some children, parents are the problem. Sam and Sara (names changed) did not have any kids. They longed for children. Eventually, they were blessed with a baby boy. A few years later, I happened to meet them again, but I was in for a surprise. Sara had become very thin. Shocked, I inquired about her health. The couple confided to me that the hyperactive behaviour of their kid was keeping them on their toes causing them lot of stress.

### Stress Caused by Natural Calamities

When natural disasters occur, they cause a lot of damage and unexpected loss. In 2017, Hurricane Irma caused about $50 billion worth of damage. Around 6.5 million Floridians were made to evacuate their homes.[5] My friend, who was caught in the exodus, called me as he sat in traffic for what wound up being twelve hours. He relayed to me how distressed his family was and how worried he was that he'd lose his home and all his belongings. Such uncertainty and feelings of helplessness naturally cause enormous stress. The COVID-19 pandemic is another example of a natural event

5 The Expensive and Lasting Damages of Hurricane Irma, Hurricanedamage.com, https://hurricanedamage.com/blog/damages-cost-hurricane-irma/#:~:text=Hurricane%20Irma%20was%20an%20expensive,property%20damage%20to%20Hurricane%20Irma.

that caused great stress to many people. Since it began, cases of anxiety, depression, substance abuse and suicide have considerably increased.[6]

## 2.2. INTERNAL FACTORS

### Stress Caused by One's Own Body and Mind

We all want a healthy body and a controlled, calm and peaceful mind. When something disturbs our body or mind for a prolonged period of time, we become stressed out. These are called personal stressors. While physical stressors are often easy to pick up on, mind-related stressors are generally harder to identify.

Lust, anger, greed, arrogance, envy and delusion are the negative emotions that bring stress and misery to the mind. Dr Richard Smith and Dr Sun Hee Kim of the University of Kentucky published an article on envy and its negative effects on physical and mental health. They found that envy is a self-destructive emotion that drains an individual's physical and mental energies. Envious people develop feelings of hostility, anger and irritability. Envy is also connected with anxiety, depression, prejudice and misery. We should be

6 National Institute of Health

careful not only with what we put into our body but also with what we allow into our minds.

Now let us look at a few of the specific factors that lead to a stress-prone mentality: self-inflicted miseries, imagination, negative self-talk, self-pity, negative thought processes, unhealthy comparisons, bad habits and, finally, lamentation of the past or fear of the future. It is noteworthy that each one of these is born in the mind.

## Self-inflicted Miseries

It is explained in the Gita that a controlled mind is the best of friends while an uncontrolled mind is the worst of enemies. Since the mind is very subtle, science has made limited progress in truly grasping it. But both scientists and spiritualists can agree that there are few things more distressing than an unruly mind. By understanding the nature of our mind, we can improve our thought processes and thus increase our levels of peace and satisfaction.

## Imagination

People tend to fantasize a lot. Sometimes, these visualizations can get extreme. For example, after a newly married couple's first argument, one of the parties might begin to think, 'What if we one day get a divorce? What will happen to our future children? Where will I go? Will people ridicule us? Maybe we're doomed!' This string of thoughts can extend on and on, even though the argument may have already ended. Rather than wildly imagining things, we should focus on doing what is needed. Being aware of the lack of solid ground for our imagination to stand on and taking practical steps to mend a situation allow us to develop a positive attitude that prevents such negativity from manifesting.

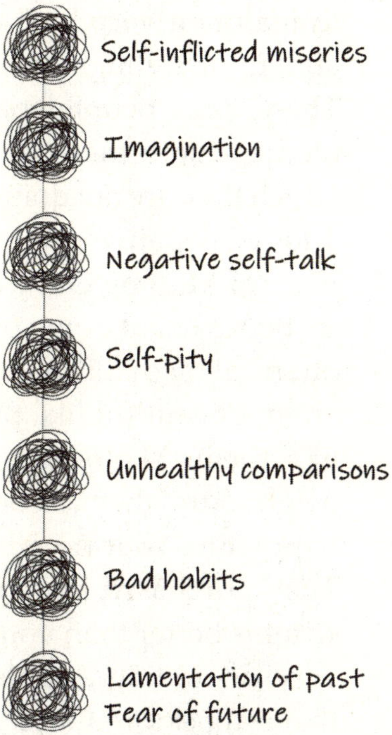


## Negative Self-talk

In this case, we begin to entertain strings of negative thoughts about ourselves. We recount all the times we failed and were demeaned before others. We recollect how we failed to live up to the expectations of mentors or parents. Many tend to maintain very high expectations of themselves and, upon failing to meet them, become miserable. These days people spend a lot of time on social media where they see their friends doing things which they are not doing. If not careful, this triggers a lot of negative self-talk. People call this FOMO (Fear of Missing Out). To save ourselves from this, it's better to cut down or totally stop spending time on social media. The sneering mind might say, 'You are not beautiful like them. You are not intelligent like them. You're not as talented. Look at your neighbours, they are better than you. They have a happy life. Your friends are doing better than you. They purchased a brand new car. Your brother or sister is better than you.' This type of inner voice is very degrading and depressing. Once we realize that setbacks and insecurities are common, we can start viewing them as stepping stones to success.

### Self-pity

Sometimes the mind sings the sad song of self-pity. Some people think all the problems of the world befall them alone. Instead of objectively addressing their own problems, they tend to only want others to show sympathy to and speak in favour of them. They always appear to be overwhelmed with worries and troubles. They must realize that such self-pity is a key reason for their problems. By not indulging it and by choosing to use their intelligence to find solutions instead of justifications for wallowing, they can progress towards success.

### Unhealthy Comparisons

There is nothing wrong with being inspired by someone. We should indeed imbibe good principles from the examples set by others. However, unhealthy comparisons trigger envy and frustration. When we cannot keep on competing, stress and anxiety are triggered. Jasmine and rose are two completely different types of flowers. While the jasmine exudes a strong and beautiful scent, its flowers aren't exceedingly beautiful. The rose has an exquisite appearance but usually gives off only a faint smell. If the jasmine bud compared its flowers with those of the rose, it would feel discouraged. If the rose compared its scent with that of the jasmine, it would feel the same way. The point is that everyone is endowed with some uniquely desirable characteristic. Instead of becoming jealous of others, we should respect them and try to learn from them while honing our own unique individuality.

### Bad Habits

To overcome stress and anxiety, many people take the shelter of bad habits. Overeating, smoking, drugs and other addictions are a few potential faulty shelters. People often become slaves to these shelters and waste their lives away. The Gita explains that anything that gives instant pleasure eventually leads to misery. We are thus warned not to fall for the tricks of temporary pleasures, the bait of quick fixes. Always remember the big picture.

### Lamentation of the Past and Fear of the Future

The mind is unsteady. It tends to either lament the things we have done in the past or worry about the things we may do in the future. All the while, the present moment continuously slips from our grasp. The solution is to remind ourselves that we can't change the past, but we can learn from it and thus better shape our future. Rather than becoming paralysed in thoughts about the future, we should get to work and do what we can to start moulding our ideal future today.

## 2.3. THE EFFECT OF STRESS ON THE BODY

Is stress all bad? Certainly not. Stress is the way the body copes with demanding situations. For an active life, stress is required. For example, when we have an interview for a new job approaching, we feel stress and, as a result, we prepare and perform well, making it much more likely that we will land the job.

This kind of productive stress is medically termed 'eustress'. Specifically, eustress refers to that stress which arises from a need to increase focus and productivity so as to achieve something. Examples include the stress associated with organizing a party, getting married, caring for a newborn, earning a promotion at work, etc.

On the other hand, there is the kind of stress that arises from a recognition that our abilities and resources are not sufficient to handle a given situation. This type of stress is called distress. Examples include the stress associated with divorce, the death of a loved one, an incurable disease, etc.

### What Happens When We Are Under Stress?

While stress is an inbuilt mechanism of the body that prepares us for different kinds of situations, prolonged stress can lead to severe health problems. These effects start in the brain. Research has shown that stress can shrink the prefrontal cortex, which is directly responsible for our memory and learning. Bodily effects are relatively easy to reverse when compared to effects on the brain. Abnormalities in the brain can also lead to additional abnormalities in the body. Headaches, sleeping disorders, anxiety disorders, depression, loneliness and increased irritability are a few issues a stressed-out person can expect to face. Stress also causes the heart to beat faster. Prolonged or frequent stress can thus cause high blood pressure.

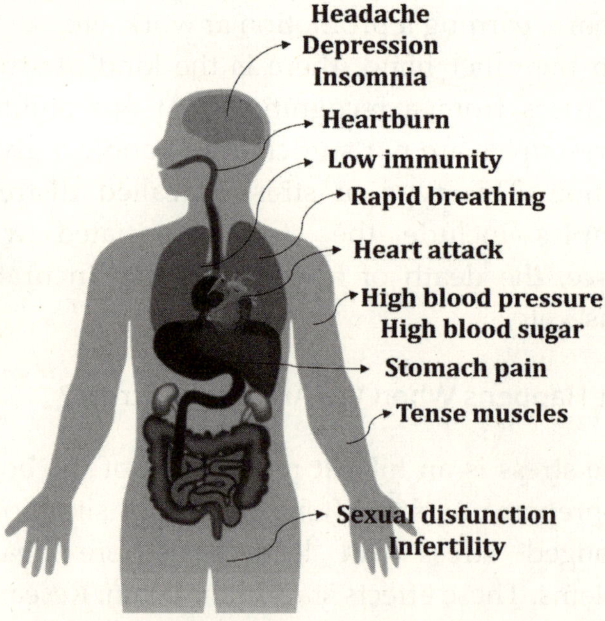

Such poor blood pressure and heart rhythms can damage the arteries and lead to a heart attack. Stress has also been known to trigger psoriasis and other skin disorders. Muscular pains and ulcers, decreased immunity and a whole slew of other potential sicknesses come into the picture as a result of prolonged stress as well.

## 2.4. THE EFFECT OF STRESS ON THE MIND

As discussed, the mind continuously stresses about what we lack and makes us miserable, causing cycles of stress that directly impact our mood and are reflected in our behaviour. These can be easily perceived when individuals under stress feel overwhelmed by anxiety, restlessness or a lack of motivation. Ultimately, they are reflected in our behaviour—uncontrolled anger, substance abuse, scrolling through social media for relief, eating too much or not eating at all. Prolonged stress can shrink the prefrontal cortex responsible for our memory and learning.

## SUMMARY

### External Factors of Stress

1. Misery caused by others
2. Misery caused by natural calamities

### Internal Factors of Stress

1. Self-inflicted miseries
2. Imagination
3. Negative self-talk
4. Self-pity
5. Unhealthy comparisons
6. Bad habits
7. Lamentation of the past and fear of the future

### Impact of Stress on the Body and Mind

Prolonged stress impacts our brain. We start suffering from headaches, sleeping disorders, anxiety problems, depression, loneliness and irritability. Stress causes the heart to beat faster, which causes high blood pressure.

Research has shown that stress can shrink the prefrontal cortex, which is directly responsible for the functioning of our memory and for learning.

## QUESTIONS

1. What internal factors cause you stress and anxiety?

______________________________________________

______________________________________________

______________________________________________

______________________________________________

2. What damage to your body and mind has stress already caused?

______________________________________________

______________________________________________

______________________________________________

______________________________________________

# CHAPTER 3

# How Can Stress Be Prevented?

## 3.1. EFFECTIVE COMMUNICATION

Relationships can be stressful. Poor communication makes matters much worse. The problem in the internet age is that everyone seems to be busy always. When we are occupied with so many things, we tend to forget to nurture certain relationships, which causes communication gaps filled with ill feelings. So, how do we improve our communication?

### Basic Communication Skills

#### *N.I.C.E.: Needs, Interests, Concerns and Expectations*

When we speak, we should keep in mind four things about the other person: their needs, interests,

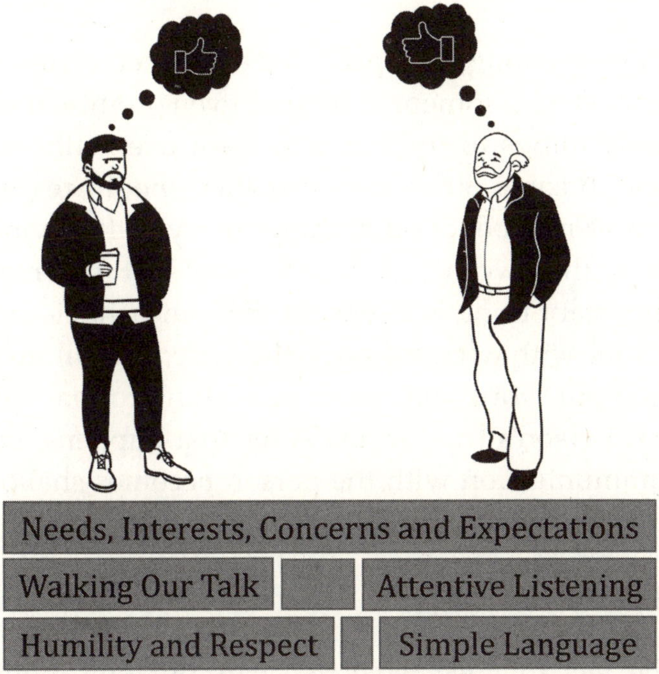


concerns and expectations. If we can address these aspects in our communication with them, we can forge and maintain a healthy relationship. We should ask: 'Am I aware of this person's needs? Am I addressing their concerns? Am I meeting their expectations?' By addressing each of these questions consistently, we can show the person we genuinely care about them and thus communicate more effectively.

### *Walk Your Talk*

It's easy enough to speak sweetly when trying to connect with someone. We may even promise them many things to try and win them over, shift our tone to come off as someone they should respect or do a number of other things to try and convince them that we are a certain way. But the most important thing is to ensure that our behaviour is in sync with what we say. Otherwise, our failure to keep our word will result in a failure to maintain that person's trust in us. After that happens, our communication with the person becomes shallow and weak.

### *Attentive Listening*

The fact that we have two ears but one mouth indicates that we should listen more than we speak. Solid communication demands that we develop a strong understanding of the person in front of us. For this, attentive listening is crucial. We should make it a point to truly internalize their needs, concerns, interests and expectations. We should sit or stand erect, showing interest in them and what they have to say. We should also make good eye contact, ask relevant questions and seek clarifications on any points that aren't completely clear.

### *Humility and Respect*

People pick up more from the feelings behind our words than from the words themselves. Once, a challenging student raised his hand before a large assembly and asked a swami on stage, 'Are you the guru of the whole world?' The swami paused for a moment. A single tear rolled down his cheek as he, with utter humility, replied, 'I am not *anyone's* guru; I am a servant of the whole world.' The audience was shocked into silence by the profundity of the swami's response. Genuine goodwill will always shine through in our communication. It is thus crucial to lead a life of honesty and integrity.

### *Simple Language*

The goal of communication is to effectively transmit our thoughts and feelings. While these thoughts and feelings can often be complicated, we should try our best to put them in simple terms so that others can clearly understand them.

## DIFFERENT FORMS OF COMMUNICATION

### Verbal Communication

Verbal communication encompasses phone/ video calls, face-to-face conversations and public speaking. Whether it is an informal friendly chat or a board meeting, effectively expressing ourselves is very important. We need to make sure the opposite party can understand our message. As mentioned before, apart from words, our body language and our tone play a vital role in communication. In both one-to-one and one-to-many conversations, attentively listening to others and understanding their needs, interests, concerns and expectations can help us communicate in an effective way.

### Non-Verbal Communication

Non-verbal communication is one of two aspects of communication that should especially be considered but is often overlooked (the other being the written, or typed, word, which will be considered next). The volume of our voice, its tone and our body language convey a massive amount of information. The face is, after all, the index of the mind. Before we even open our mouths, people can pick up on the kind of message we're about to relay based on our facial expressions. When there is enthusiasm in the voice of the speaker, they tend to believe in what they are saying, and, often, the listeners too start to believe in it. On the other hand, someone who speaks hesitatingly, looking around the room nervously, will not be very convincing. So, be sure to consider the message you're conveying at a non-verbal level and make sure it lines up with your goal in speaking.

### Written Communication

In the internet age, written communication is of the utmost importance. One, because it is our most-used form of communication, and two, because it has been enshrined in the World Wide Web. By ensuring emails, texts, e-contracts and the like are properly written, we can be very effective in our online exchanges. On the other hand, failing to be thorough in these areas can lead to enormous miscommunications and even ruined relationships. One should also note that it can be very difficult to convey one's mood through the written word. One should take a moment after writing important messages to ensure they cannot be misconstrued by the receiving party.

## MISCELLANEOUS POINTERS FOR EFFECTIVE COMMUNICATION

Books can be (and have been) written about each form of communication discussed here; such is the importance of this topic. Let me close by listing nine ways of communicating effectively:

1. When someone is speaking, we should allow them to finish. We should not interrupt them abruptly and start laying our points on top of theirs. This conveys to the other person that we are disregarding not only their message but also them, in entirety.
2. We need to maintain comfortable eye contact with the speaker. This conveys to the speaker that we are paying attention. Also, we need to observe the body language of the speaker. We should not, however, constantly stare at the speaker. This may cause them discomfort.
3. Communication is not a product; it is a process. We need to constantly maintain good relationships with others. For that to happen, we need to fulfil our promises and commitments to them.
4. Be an active listener. Try repeating the sentences of others by saying, 'If I understood correctly, you said [...].' Leaning forward, taking notes and asking questions are a few signs that we are listening attentively. Our posture is very important. We should not be cross-armed—that shows we are on the defensive.

5. We need to be mentally ready to assert our opinions when needed. Our message should be very clear. To that end, write down all the points that support your position.
6. We should be okay with people having opinions that differ from our own. We should not react emotionally. This creates stress. This also creates an environment of distrust. We must target the problem, not the person. People view the problem from so many different angles. Even if we do not agree with another's opinion, we should agree to disagree and move forward. In this way, we can maintain cordial relationships with others.
7. Speaking confidently before others requires sense control and practice. Good preparation and handy notes help.
8. At the workplace, conveying a clear message to the right person at the right time is important. This prevents confusion.
9. If we organize meetings, we need to clearly convey the venue, date, and time of the meetings to all participants well in advance. Meetings should start on time and end on time. We should explain the rules and regulations of the meeting along with the

responsibilities of the participants at the beginning of the meeting. That way we make sure each meeting goes smoothly. We should focus on only the agenda for discussion and not allow any distractions. We thus allocate specific time periods for each point on the agenda. Usually, one person records the minutes of the meeting.

### 3.2. TIME MANAGEMENT

William Penn said that time is what we want the most, but what we utilize the worst. If we want to lead a stress-free life, we need to understand the power of time. The European paradigm views time in the form of years, months, days, minutes and seconds. It is often thought of in terms of periods within which we want to pursue and attain certain goals and objectives. However, Eastern wisdom considers time to be a powerful, active energy. When Robert Oppenheimer, the director of the first nuclear bomb project, witnessed his nuclear weapon create a mushroom cloud that stretched into the heavens, he made a statement **'Now I am become Death, the destroyer of worlds'** that referenced a characterization of time in the Bhagavad Gita: 'Time I am, the great destroyer of all the worlds.' (*Bhagavad Gita*, 11.32).

A mosquito lives a life of one week. During its first day, it grows dramatically. On its second day, it goes to school to learn how to tactfully bite and suck blood without disturbing humans and how to take off without being killed. On the third day, it finds a mate and becomes a father to some 100 baby mosquitoes. On the fourth, fifth and sixth days, it enjoys family life with its mate and children, giving the new critters the same life lessons it received just a couple of days prior to their birth. It is very busy all the time. But it does not realize that its body is becoming weaker and weaker; finally, on the seventh day, having lived a full life, it is taken over by old age. It lies down to die.

There are around 2,500 species in this world that live for only one day. The fly lives for only four weeks, mice only one or two years. Cats and dogs generally live for twelve to fourteen years. If you analyse their lives, regardless of the circumstances, all these species focus on spending their time doing only four basic things: eating, sleeping, mating and defending themselves from danger. If they do these four things well throughout their life, they can consider themselves very successful. However, human life is meant to be different. If we analyse our lives, we find that we too spend most of our time doing the same basic things that animals do, but, internally, there is a world of difference.

We can utilize human life to explore the subtleties of human existence. Science explains the functioning of the universe but cannot explain the purpose of our life or of the existence of the universe.

Why was this universe created? Why were *we* created? Why do miseries befall us? Why does weather trouble us? Why are pandemics imposed on us? Why should people experience stress, anxiety, depression and other disorders? Why can't I remain youthful forever? Why must I become old and, finally, die? Who is behind the functioning of this universe? Is there unlimited and non-stop happiness? Think about it. Only we can ask such questions, not the other animals on this planet.

***

Eastern wisdom tells us the story of a king who once decided to pay a salary to the craziest person in his kingdom. He conducted interviews to identify the craziest person and then started paying him the promised amount. Eventually, the king suffered a brain haemorrhage and the doctors told him he had very little time to live and that now was the time to take care of all his remaining responsibilities. When he heard the news, he was shocked. He knew there was something *called* death. He had witnessed it in the lives of his elder relatives. But he had been so caught up with worldly pursuits that he had never paid any serious attention to death as an inevitable event in his own life, too. He had never thought it would come so quickly. He was not ready for it. In a panic, he immediately started delegating his powers to others and attending to his final responsibilities. Suddenly, he thought of the insane man and called for him. The following conversation ensued.

King: The doctors told me I am going to die very soon.

Crazy Man: What is dying?

King: You are crazy, you won't understand. Basically, death means a person goes on a long journey and never returns. Now I am going on that long journey and will not return.

Crazy Man: Oh, okay. In that case, be sure to take with you all the hard-earned wealth, jewellery and other riches that you have earned during your lifetime.

King: On this journey, no one can take any physical assets with them.

Crazy Man: You have so many queens who have given their lives to you, and you have given your life to them. You have so many children for whom you worked so hard. Please take them with you. They will be of great help during this voyage.

King: They cannot accompany me on this journey. I have to go alone. I must leave everything behind.

Crazy Man: What about your great name and fame? You've spent a lifetime establishing your reputation.

King: Nothing. Anyway, I called you to tell you that my son will continue to pay your salary after my departure, so don't worry about your future.

Crazy Man: I cannot work any longer. I am resigning from my position.

King: Ummm, alright, well, find another crazy man and let us know whom you choose. We will pay the salary to him.

Crazy Man: As I see it, *you* are that crazy man.

King (shocked): Why me?

Crazy Man: You knew you would have to go on this journey one day. You knew you couldn't take anything with you. Still, you equated your time with money and worked so hard to acquire all these riches. You knew well that no one could come with you. Yet, you spent all your time with your near and dear family members. You knew about this big journey, but you never made a single preparation for it. Now you are completely unprepared. That is why you are so afraid now. I consider this craziness.

What the 'crazy man' said opened the king's eyes. He fully realized his mistake. Regardless of one's wealth and influence, the body is a living thing, and, like any other living thing, it expires in time. Along with taking care of the body and the people connected with it, we also need to prepare for our final journey. We need to acquire assets that we can take with us during our final journey.

Technology has revolutionized our lives. We have access to 500 television and online channels at the press of a button. We can see our relatives on the other side of the planet. We can reach anyone at any time using our smart phones. We can inquire about any subject and we always have all kinds of information at our fingertips. But what do we use this technology for? Generally, we use it for the same eating, sleeping, mating and defending functions that other animals perform. Perhaps we do so in a more refined way, but the activities are the same at a fundamental level.

When Alexander the Great was on an invasion spree with his army, a thief broke into his camps and started stealing things before finally getting caught by Alexander's soldiers. When he was brought before Alexander, the latter ordered his soldiers to kill the thief as punishment for attempted theft. The thief retorted by claiming that Alexander had no authority or right to award capital punishment. A little surprised, Alexander asked him to explain. The thief contended that there was practically no difference between them. 'You have a huge army and with them you conquer kingdoms, kill people who oppose you and steal all their riches. I am alone. I come in the night and steal whatever I can get. You are a big thief and I am a small thief. Since we are both are thieves and are involved in the same activity, the big thief has no right to kill the small thief.' Alexander saw truth in this argument and ordered the small thief's release.[7]

In a similar way, the fact that we have sophisticated systems and an advanced sense of enjoyment does not mean that our eating, mating, sleeping and defending is any better than that of other animals. We need to have a material life. We need wealth to cater to the needs of our family.

---

7 'Story:Alexander–theGreatthief!',Divinemindfulness.com, https://divinemindfulness.com/story-alexander-the-great-thief/; 'Story: Alexander–The Great Thief', Akṛṣṇadevotee.wordpress.com, https://akrsnadevotee.wordpress.com/2020/08/14/story-alexander-the-great-thief/

We need to have a social life. We need to spend time with family members, friends and relatives. However, Vedic wisdom teaches us that, essentially, we are souls. Thus, we need to nurture ourselves through spirituality. We need to allocate some time in our day to cleansing our heart and reaching our sacred space of happiness, beyond the body.

If we cultivate the habit of cleansing our heart and inhabiting our sacred space, we can experience peace for some amount of time every day. At least during the period of time we set aside for it, we remain untouched by the problems of our life. This is exactly like sitting in a boat amidst waves that represent stressful life situations. As we go deeper into our internal spiritual life, we develop more experience and maturity in handling stressful situations. This is exactly like an expert boatman manoeuvring the boat through waves. The stormy nature of the world will not change. Our ability to manoeuvre the boat certainly will. Our ability to address these stressful situations improves as we go forth on the path of spirituality.

Balancing the material and social aspects of life with spirituality is the foundational principle of time management. Of course, to achieve this balance, we need to lead an honest life, not for others but for our own integrity. Also, by leading an honest life, we set a good example for future generations.

For more information on how to manage time, please refer to the chapters on Time Management.

### 3.3. ANXIETY MANAGEMENT

I know a girl who gets severely anxious whenever a fly enters her room. She is terrified of flying insects. Her eyes remain glued to the bug as it surveys the room. Another small child I know is scared of spiders—she becomes frozen in terror whenever one appears. Others feel the same way before a public speaking engagement, while still others become incapacitated by their fear of failing important exams. What is fear anyway? At a basic level, fear or anxiety arises from feeling a lack of control over one's situation. The world is arranged in such a way that we can only control so much; the rest is a matter of fate. Below are a few techniques I've found effective in coping with the unknown.

#### Pep Talks

When you are suddenly nervous or overcome by anxiety, one way to rise above it is to remember all of the previous occasions on which you dealt with similar circumstances and emerged safe and secure. You can talk yourself up by recalling your knowledge and abilities and how they've gotten you through similarly difficult situations before. What makes this time any different? Accept the challenge as one that will help you become even more resilient in dealing with whatever kind of issue may be at hand.

## Knowledge

Vedic wisdom teaches us that we are not this body of bones, flesh and blood, but a divine being within the machine. This also means that we are not our brain—the source of our anxiety. As a particle of spirit, each of us has infinitely more power than the matter around us. By positively meditating on our eternal nature along with the temporary

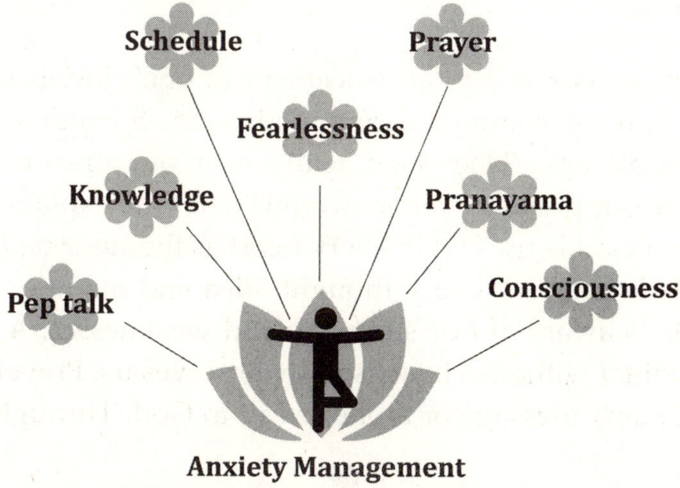

nature of the body and the material world around us, we can kindle the flame of empowerment and shed our anxiety.

### Fearlessness

By failing to identify with our true, eternal, spiritual nature, we leave ourselves no choice but to become absorbed in bodily consciousness. Deep absorption in the idea that 'I am this body' understandably causes fear. After all, what could be more threatening than being forever damaged or incapacitated, as can sometimes happen to the body. By instead identifying with the soul, we can reduce the intensity of all fears related to the body, allowing us to better face any apparently fearful situation.

### Prayer

Prayer is a key to advancement in one's life. It is a way of communicating with God. Sometimes people ask, 'Does God really hear our prayers? Are our prayers ever answered?' The Gita explains that God is present in every heart as the *super soul*. He knows our every thought, idea and intention. He is aware of our strengths and weaknesses. As a silent witness, He constantly observes us. Prayer is a text message or a phone call to God. Through our prayer, we convey our emotions to Him. Even though there is no prescribed way of praying, we can pray in our own way to communicate our feelings or borrow the prayers of noble persons of the past and present.

Initially, we may ask God to fulfil our material needs and ambitions. But, as we progress in life, we come to realize the temporary nature of everything in this world. Considering this realization, it is wise to go beyond treating God as a supplier of our material comforts. To sustain our relationship with God, it is important we lead an honest and prayerful life. As we mature, instead of seeking material gains, we seek His guidance, His help in purifying our hearts and providing us the strength to overcome moral weaknesses and make appropriate decisions.

### Pranayama

Pranayama is a medically verified means of reducing anxiety. As a refresher, whenever you're feeling imbalanced, take a moment to inhale deeply, hold your breath for five seconds, exhale completely and leave the lungs empty for a few moments before inhaling again. While so doing, try to become conscious of the flow of air into and out of your body. Take the opportunity to remind yourself of your nature as a spiritual soul within a material body.

### Mantra Meditation

Mantra meditation is a form of meditation that can immediately quell anxiety. Find a quiet and personal space. Close your eyes and say aloud, 'Ra-ma.' Try repeating it slowly to yourself a few times, becoming conscious of the sound vibration as you create it. Repeat the mantra 'Rama' to yourself with an attentive mind whenever anxiety appears.

### Schedule

If we have a daily schedule of planned activities and we follow our schedule, we constantly provide our mind with a productive engagement that keeps it occupied in a healthy way. Being idle or being alone is not a good thing for someone experiencing anxiety.

### Elevation of the Consciousness

Incapacitating feelings like anxiety are symptoms of the mode of darkness (tamas). We will discuss modes of nature in the coming chapter. Overcome tamas by maintaining a clean and healthy lifestyle, exercising regularly, maintaining a steady schedule of eating and sleeping and developing a routine of daily meditation.

## SUMMARY

### Principles of Effective Communication

1. Needs, interests, concerns and expectations (N.I.C.E.)
2. Walk Your Talk
3. Attentive listening
4. Humility and Respect
5. Simple language

### Anxiety Management

1. Pep talks
2. Knowledge
3. Fearlessness
4. Prayer
5. Pranayama
6. Mantra meditation
7. Schedule
8. Elevation of the consciousness

### QUESTIONS

1. When was the last time you felt the need to improve your communication skills?

________________________________________

________________________________________

________________________________________

________________________________________

2. Which principles of communication from among those discussed in this chapter most struck you?

________________________________________

________________________________________

________________________________________

________________________________________

3. What solutions will you employ to overcome anxiety?

________________________________________

________________________________________

________________________________________

________________________________________

CHAPTER

# 4

# How Can Stress Be Managed?

## 4.1. MANAGING STRESS AT THE LEVELS OF BODY AND MIND

### Body

Properly managing our body, mind and soul is essential to managing stress. Our body is a marvellous machine with 206 bones and 100,000 miles worth of blood vessels. For it to function efficiently, there needs to be a constant flow of blood from the heart to each and every part of the body. To this end, the body requires proper maintenance. Besides a healthy diet, proper exercise is absolutely essential. Generating physical stress through exercise naturally helps subdue mental stress. Putting our body under physical stress triggers the release of endorphins that act as mood stabilizers and painkillers. Serotonin is also generated along with other hormones that help relieve anxiety and depression. If you're not one for the gym, you can get your fill of exercise through yoga, tai chi, long walks in the park, swimming or various other forms of physical engagement.

As previously mentioned, it is crucial to maintain a healthy schedule of eating and sleeping. By so doing, one enters a bodily rhythm that makes it easier for things like digestion and rejuvenation to take place. As discussed in the Time Management section, by failing to plan, we plan to fail. Make a plan that allows your body to sync up with nature. Maintaining healthy eating and sleeping habits will ensure that the mind feels less bogged down by bodily troubles and becomes more peaceful.

Refraining from unhealthy activities is also a part of maintaining the machine. Alcohol, smoking and illicit sexual relationships may appear to relieve us from stress and give us momentary happiness, but they eventually make us slaves, causing lot of stress. It is very difficult to relinquish these vices. Replacing these with good and healthy relationships is the key. Happiness, when shared with others, increases; distress, when shared with others, decreases. When we face a problem, if we share it with others, we feel relieved. We have all experienced that simply sharing what is in our hearts reduces its burden. Sometimes we may receive good advice. We can share our problems with our near and dear ones. For this to happen, we need to have loving relationships with our family members and friends.

The Gita says that the regulation of the body can be achieved by worshiping the divine and offering respect to pious people like one's spiritual teacher and superiors like one's parents. Cleanliness, simplicity, celibacy and non-violence help regulate the body. The above principles, when followed carefully, will carve out a mindset capable of facing any adversity or miserable situation in life.

### Mind

Because the mind is subtler than the body, it is much more difficult to maintain. Our minds tend towards negativity; the word 'mind' stands for 'magnify, imagine, negativity, deny'. It magnifies small problems to scare us, imagines things worse than they are to discourage us, is attracted to negativity and denies us opportunities for personal growth. While not everyone feels these effects to the same degree, the tendencies can be found in everyone's mind. To counteract these proclivities, there are a few techniques one may employ:

### *Look at the Bright Side*

My guru Radhanath Swami once said, 'In every moment of suffering there is the seed of a blessing to come.' Usually we are so overwhelmed with the suffering, we don't recognize the blessing we are going to receive. Whenever I went through some calamity, I patiently waited for the blessing to come. It always came in a form that I could recognize. There is always a light at the end of the tunnel. Sometimes we must patiently make our way through darkness to eventually see the light.

### *Be Aware of the Temporary Nature of Everything*

Do you remember who won the Olympic gold in gymnastics in 2004 or the team that won the World Cup the same year? What is history anyway? It is nothing but the stories of people long gone or soon to be so. A teacher once asked their students what Alexander the Great, Abraham Lincoln and George Washington all had in common. One witty student got up and said, 'They're all dead and gone.' Even the greatest achievers in history met their ends. From this, we may conclude that *everything* is temporary—the good as well as the bad. When we understand and realize the temporary nature of every material thing—may it be a relationship, a car, a mansion, a gadget, or name and fame—we are not very distressed when we lose it. But today's civilization is all about acquiring positions and possessions to become joyful. Sadly, we are all brainwashed to believe that these things will bring unlimited joy. But the reality is different. Hence, it is imperative to have a spiritual point of view. Then, we will have the eyes of knowledge to see the truth. Then, we will become more and more stress-free.

### *Live for Yourself*

People buy expensive cars and palatial mansions to try and make themselves happy, but often they just become more depressed. Many people lead their entire lives trying to do and say things that they think will impress others. Their attempts to forge an identity in this manner lead to their losing themselves completely. How can we be happy just by pretending to be so? The fact is, happiness is a state of consciousness, not a state of affairs. Instead of seeking external validation, try to feel good about yourself by maintaining an impeccable character based on the ideals you hold dear.

### *Sense Control*

The more we think of opportunities for sense enjoyment, the more the mind becomes dissatisfied. This may come in the form of sexual desires, desires for certain kinds of food, for social status or positions of authority or anything else that may give us a sense of sensual or egoistic pleasure. If we provide our senses whatever they ask for, then, like spoilt children, they go out of control. Instead, we should reasonably regulate them and not allow the mind to be controlled by their whims. The example below explains the importance of sense control in one's life. In the now-famous marshmallow experiment[8] demonstrating the value of self-regulation, psychologist Walter Mischel found that the ability of four-year-olds to resist one marshmallow for fifteen minutes translated to higher SAT scores thirteen years later, higher college completion rates after twenty years and significantly higher income after thirty years.

Ancient yogis were known for their exceptional powers. They generated these powers through celibacy, mindfulness, silence, meditation and

---

8 Standford Marshmallow Experiment, Wikipedia, https://en.wikipedia.org/wiki/Stanford_marshmallow_experiment

austere spiritual practices. Focusing on spiritual thoughts, spiritual duties and the welfare of others made their minds flexible and ready to adjust to any situation. Our life is run by our thoughts. By altering our thought process, we can improve the landscape of life. However, we need to systematically train our mind to actually alter its functioning.

### *Simplicity*

Simplicity means the absence of duplicity. By developing a non-duplicitous mind, we can simplify and essentialize our lives. Here are four practical steps we can take to whip the mind into shape:

#### LESS SHOPPING

Ours is a world of consumerism. 'Buy. Buy. Buy.' Instead, question the need to buy. Don't allow yourself to become an impulsive buyer. Don't be tempted by deals. You may be able to afford it, but the planet cannot. Before buying anything, please meditate on this one question: 'Do I really need this?' Also, please meditate on the health of the planet. Consumerism is one of the main reasons for the ill health of the planet. We don't need a lot of stuff. After some time, most of the stuff we buy ends up in the basement anyway. When we indulge the tendency to buy, use and toss items, we develop a 'use and throw' mentality and apply the same thought process to our relationships. Thus, in order to truly enjoy a stress-free life with friends and family, we need to buy less. This will save us time, money and energy.

### AVOID TIME WASTERS

We can cut out things that are not important to us. Why should we invest in them when they are neither important nor urgent? Watching TV for long hours, spending time on social media sites, browsing on smartphones and long gossipy phone calls is a waste. If we can cut down on these activities, we can conserve a lot of energy and time that can instead be utilized for constructive things. We then learn to say 'no' to others and keep free time for ourselves.

### CULTIVATE SPIRITUALITY

Science explains the functioning of the universe but fails to explain the goal of the universe. If we carefully observe this world, we'll notice happiness and misery come and go like changing seasons. Who is behind all the uncertainties of this world? Everything in the world is temporary. No one here is immune to stress and suffering. This fact encourages us to search for the absolute truth and pursue the path of spirituality. The goal of spirituality is to cleanse the heart and awaken the peace and joy within. Once all the impurities are removed, we can share this innate peace and love with others.

One time, I went to see a senior monk to seek some advice. We sat next to a lake for a discussion of the topic at hand. As soon as the senior monk sat, the fish in the pond began jumping six feet into the air one after another after another—out of sheer happiness that the monk was close to them! I was astonished. On another occasion, a deer in a forest saw the same monk and started following him, attracted by his loving demeanour. Usually, deer are very timid and run at the sight of humans. But when the heart is pure and filled with joy, you see the hand of God in every situation.

## DO NOT OVERLOAD YOUR SCHEDULE

Keep your schedule simple. Also, make sure you have free time for personal growth in your planner. Introspection is a part of personal growth. Honest introspection reveals dark spots in our life. If our schedule is overloaded, we may not have free time for ourselves. Please learn to delegate or eliminate unimportant tasks. That way, you can focus on important tasks and still have free time.

## 4.2. KNOW YOURSELF

### Modes of Nature

Each one of us acts differently at different times due to the influence of nature's subtle forces. We have all, on many occasions, thought, 'I should not have done that.' Sometimes, we act against our will as if someone is forcing us to act a certain way. Nature is very powerful. It acts on everyone and everything at all times. The Bhagavad Gita calls these forces of nature the three gunas or modes of material nature. They are called gunas (ropes) because of their binding property. Based on our mindset and our choices, we are influenced by a particular mode or combination of modes at every moment.

The three modes are goodness (sattva), passion (rajas) and ignorance (tamas). These are purely technical terms, and one should not think of them according to the literal meanings of goodness, passion and ignorance.

In art, the primary colours are red, blue and yellow. But when we mix these three in different proportions, we can get an unlimited number of colours. In a similar way, when the three modes are mixed, they generate an unlimited number of different mindsets and activities. A calm and peaceful natural trail filled with varieties of trees and plants is in the mode of goodness, the stock exchange is in the mode of passion, bars are in the mode of ignorance. The mode of goodness prevails in the early morning, the mode of passion takes over in the afternoon and the mode of ignorance dominates at night.

The first guna, the mode of goodness, is illuminating. Those who are under its influence want to lead a life of purity. They practise self-restraint and sense control to stay away from vices and bad habits. For this reason, they lead happy lives. They understand their weaknesses and strengths. People who develop the mode of goodness become wise and stress-free. They strive to advance in terms of both material and spiritual knowledge. They are not debilitated by misery. People of this nature are usually charitable and find happiness in helping others. Such people also keep themselves very clean, often observe plant-based diets, treat others with respect and handle life's problems with thoughtfulness and care.

Individuals in the mode of goodness are distinguished by the following characteristics:

- They have a high spiritual quotient.
- They have good control of their senses.
- They make decisions after thoughtful deliberation.
- They spend lot of time planning.
- They maintain their cool in all circumstances.
- They remain alert.
- They possess immense mental and spiritual strength.
- They possess a resolute determination to attain their objectives.

The second guna is the mode of passion. Persons who are influenced by this mode have unlimited desires. They want fame, prestige and honour in society. They are very ambitious and want to acquire possessions and attain positions in this world. If there is no personal gain at stake, they don't feel inspired to perform. They are driven to achieve goal after goal. Even after achieving a lot and making their mark, they remain dissatisfied. They have a very competitive nature, and when they see someone doing better than them, they find it difficult to accept. They possess a strong 'I, me, mine' mentality. For this reason, they are often stressed out despite their best attempts to remain cool. This mode also results in a strong sex drive in both men and women.

Individuals in the mode of passion exhibit the following tendencies:

- They are very driven and goal-oriented.
- They are very hard-working and possess both physical and mental vitality.
- They are known to lead the way in finding solutions to problems.
- Their self-centredness creates problems with people of a similar nature.
- They are known to push themselves to the point of exhaustion.

The third guna is the mode of ignorance. People influenced by this mode tend to be very lazy and sleep much more than required. They are very fond of intoxication. They don't know right from wrong. They do things that are harmful to their own self-interest. They tend to be envious and wrathful. They pick up bad habits easily and have difficulty giving them up. When they encounter problems, they tend to develop self-pity. They're often prone to depression, anxiety and sometimes suicide.

Individuals in the mode of ignorance possess the following traits:

- They adopt an escapist mentality to deal with difficult situations.
- They are frequently driven by negative emotions.
- Amidst problems, they become confused, feel self-pity and look for external support.
- They have very limited control over themselves.
- They take the shelter of alcohol and other intoxicants as 'solutions' to their problems in life.

Below are some suggestions for individuals affected by each of the three modes of nature:

### Stress Management Suggestions for Those in the Mode of Goodness

Though people in the mode of goodness are said to be cool, there is no pure goodness in this world. The mode of goodness is always mixed with passion and ignorance in different proportions. Moreover, the world is designed to ensure that everyone runs into unexpected frustrations. Here are a few suggestions for people in the mode of goodness:

### *Dietary and Sleeping Habits*

Good dietary habits are very important to maintaining a stress-free and healthy life. Different kinds of vegetarian and vegan food are the most nourishing. The yoga texts tell us that vegetarian food increases the influence of the mode of goodness, one's lifespan, strength and overall health. Sufficient rest and undisturbed sleep at night are also crucial to leading a stress-free life. According to ayurveda, each hour of sleep clocked before midnight is equal to two hours. Between 12 a.m. and 4 a.m., each hour of sleep is equal to one hour. After 4 a.m., every hour of sleep is equal to only half an hour.[9] Hence, sleeping early and rising early after sufficient sleep will rejuvenate our body. The moral is going to bed before midnight is good for our health.

9 Ashley Zlatopolsky, 'Sorry, Night Owls: The Sleep You're Missing Before Midnight Is Crucial—Here's Why', Realsimple.com, 30 January 2023, Ashley Zlatopolsky, https://www.realsimple.com/health/preventative-health/sleep/sleep-before-midnight

| Symptoms of Mode of Goodness | Symptoms of Mode of Passion | Symptoms of Mode of Ignorance |
|---|---|---|
| Spend lot of time planning. Make decisions after thoughtful deliberation | Very driven and goal oriented | Adopt an escapist mentality amidst difficult situations |
| Have high spiritual quotient. Possess immense mental and spiritual strength | Very hardworking and possess both physical and mental vitality | Frequently driven by negative emotions |
| Remain alert. Maintain their cool in all circumstances | Finds a solution amidst problems | Confused amidst problems, feel self-pity and look for external support |
| Have good control over their senses | Their self-centeredness creates problems with people of similar nature | Very weak control over themselves |
| Possess a resolute determination to attain their objectives | Known to push themselves to the point of exhaustion | Take shelter of alcohol and other intoxicants as solutions to problems in life |

### *Stick to the Script*

These days, there are so many distractions. However, if we stick to our schedule with discipline, we progress towards a stress-free life. Making a schedule is easy; following one is difficult. Perseverance in sticking to the schedule makes a big difference.

### *Yoga, Pranayama and Mantra Meditation*

Performing yoga daily for twenty to thirty minutes also makes a big difference. Sun salutations and other yoga asanas are reliable ways of maintaining a healthy body. Pranayama's various breathing techniques, when practised on a regular basis, help us regulate and control the mind. As a result, we feel a drop in stress. Research has shown that breathing exercises can regulate the nervous system and improve our focus.

'Man' means mind, 'tra' means to liberate.[10] Mantras deliver our mind from stress. Mantras are Sanskrit words that, when repeated regularly, have a tangible calming effect on the mind. The mind is like a mirror. Our mirror-like mind is covered with dirt because of our unsavoury desires, wrongdoings and false notions. Mantras

10 Vedabase, https://vedabase.io/en/

can penetrate through all this dirt, reach the mind and cleanse the impurities that plague it. Of all the different types of meditations I've tried, I found mantra meditation to be the most sound and effective.

## Stress Management Suggestions for Those in the Mode of Passion

### *Give Up the 'I am the Doer' Mentality*

Today, everyone thinks 'I am the doer.' But we have all had diverse experiences of 'doing'; in some endeavours, even if we only put in only a little effort, we get wonderful results, while in others, even if we work extremely hard, we are unable to find any success. We have all experienced this. The yoga texts state that all we can do is try our best; the results are decided by higher forces. When we truly understand this fact, getting the desired result makes us grateful to that higher power. At other times, when we do not get the desired result despite our best efforts, we either wait for a more opportune moment or try again with vigour and enthusiasm, hoping that things will turn out differently. This type of mentality saves us from stress, anxiety and frustration.

### *Self-awareness*

Relationships can cause a lot of stress. Self-awareness is a very important quality one has to cultivate to reduce the probability of stress arising in one's relationships. People tend to think and behave as though they are the centre of the universe. If we learn to analyse our emotions and actions and how they affect others, we become cautious in our dealings with others. In fact, it is said that the size of the soul is 10,000th part of the tip of a hair strand. When we understand this fact, we become humble, and giving respect to others is the natural quality of humility. Respect also commands respect. When we respect others, they feel enlivened in our association. This will help build constructive relationships and thus save us from a lot of stress.

### *Value-based Life*

Most people try to convince others that they are happy by showing off their acquisitions and achievements. This creates lot of stress. We cannot impress anyone with our possessions or position for long. People may externally show reverence and appreciation, but internally many will boil with envy and negativity. There are so many examples of this in history. Nicolas Fouquet, the Finance Minister in the court of the French King Louis XIV, built a magnificent palace and invited King Louis for the inauguration. Upon seeing the gorgeous palace, King Louis was so inflamed with envy that he threw Nicolas in prison and built the incredible Palace of Versailles.[11] This palace then became an object of envy for all the kings of Europe. All of these kings eventually grew old, died and left this world. Instead of impressing others, if we adopt a value-based approach to life, we will feel satisfaction knowing that we pursued values instead of trying to impress people.

### *Slow Down*

Most people work very hard to achieve one goal after another, without any breaks. After a task is accomplished, they feel proud of themselves and look for adoration from others. Rather than searching for joy in a succession of such solitary achievements, we should learn to find joy in working with others to achieve our goals. It is

11 'Sun King Louis XIV of France: 24 Facts and History', Snippets of Paris, https://snippetsofparis.com/sun-king-louis-xiv/; 'NICOLAS FOUQUET - THE RIVAL OF LOUIS XIV', Youtube, 10.55, https://www.youtube.com/watch?v=tZF2EPCeGaw

important to take breaks and reconsider our lifestyle. During such breaks, spending time in nature helps ease our stress. We should always strive for self-assessment and eliminate all the unwanted stuff in life.

### *Improve Your Listening Skills*

More important than the art of speaking is the art of listening. God has given us one mouth and two ears. The message is clear: talk only when needed and listen more than you speak. If we note the points being mentioned and ask questions when others are speaking to us, they'll understand that we are attentive to their feelings. Also, repeating parts of what someone says helps them feel we've understood them correctly; it is thus a good way of connecting with and ultimately winning over them.

### *Find Joy in Selfless Service*

Performing selfless community service on a regular basis without expecting any reward or remuneration can be a great form of stress relief. There is immense joy in service and giving. This unique joy makes the heart grow wide and deep. Such a full and big heart can then serve as a cushion against stress. In one study, it was found that volunteering helps improve physical and mental health; after all, while volunteering, we are being physically and mentally active. Also, we make many new connections and establish new relationships. All these factors help reduce our stress levels.

### *Develop a Sense of Humour*

Mark Twain once said that the human race's most effective weapon was laughter. It is widely known that humour can help give us relief from stress. Humour relieves inner tension and makes us happy from within. When we laugh, we forget everything for a while and erupt in joy. Our spirits are lifted and stress is thus forced to withdraw. According to Rod Martin from the University of Western Ontario and Herbert Lefcourt from the University of Waterloo, 'humor and laughter play important roles in the maintenance of both psychological and physiological health and wellbeing in the face of stress.'[12] They were able to prove that people who

12 'Sense of humor as a moderator between stressors and moods', *Journal of Personality and Social Psychology*, Vol 45, No. 6, pp. 1313–1324, https://www.researchgate.net/publication/247434522_Sense_of_humor_as_a_moderator_between_stressors_and_moods

have greater capacities for humour recover from stress and anxiety faster than others.

In a study that sought to ascertain the effectiveness of humour as a complementary therapy for cancer patients, conducted by Bennett, McCann, Rosenberg and Zeller, it was found that those who had a well-developed sense of humour exhibited increased immune functioning. Overall, the inclusion of humour in one's day-to-day experience of life correlates with the lowering of stress levels.

### Stress Management Suggestions for Those in the Mode of Ignorance

Cut down the activities of Quadrant 4, which, as has been detailed in the section on Time Management, is the quadrant of waste and features all the activities that are neither important nor urgent. When activities are neither important nor urgent, we should neglect them. As we saw in Time Management, managers who do not plan well end up spending excessive amounts of time in Quadrant 1, the quadrant of urgent and important activities. At the end of the day, they are so exhausted and stressed out, having worked on one urgent thing after other, that they take shelter in their TV or in some other mind-numbing activity. To avoid this stressful situation, they should spend quality time in Quadrant 2, the quadrant of planning. They will then be able to work in a much more relaxed state of mind and find time to spend with family members and engage in other activities that yield long-term returns.

### *Cut Down on Procrastination*

Procrastination is one of the qualities associated with the mode of ignorance. Human life is rare and precious. How can we avoid wasting large chunks of it procrastinating? Determine a timeline for each task and adhere to it. When we develop a timeline for a task and finish that task on time, we get the immense satisfaction of having completed the task in a timely manner. This also boosts self-confidence. To this end, we should eliminate all distractions as far as possible; this means disconnecting from social media, texting, WhatsApp and the like. Ideally, all notifications should be turned off.

### *Deadlines*

Set deadlines for everything you do. Assign a date of completion to each task and review your progress on a weekly basis. If you find you are falling short, borrow time from other areas and finish the tasks.

Usually, we can borrow time from Quadrant 4 or Quadrant 3 (urgent but unimportant activities). Fear is one of the reasons for procrastination. If you find a daunting task too difficult to handle, you should either look for help or break the task up into smaller parts and complete them one after the other.

### *Develop Your SQ (Spiritual Quotient)*

We are essentially spiritual beings occupying human bodies for a few years. When the spiritual being leaves the body, it is either cremated or buried. Our presence in this body and the world is temporary. Once we understand this fact, it will take us to the next question: what is the purpose of life? When we realize we are only one of the 7.6 billion people on earth, we become humble. A century ago, our needs were very simple: food, clothing and shelter. If you ask anyone what their needs are today, what do they say? Focused on their computer and cell phone, they may not even hear your question as they ask you for a charger and the WiFi password. Author Dave Ramsey said, 'We buy things we don't need with money we don't have to impress people we don't like.' We have a moral responsibility to leave a legacy for future generations. By focusing more on spiritual development than on needless material development, we fulfil our responsibilities, both to ourselves as human beings and to future generations. This will help us develop a value-based life that will diminish our stress.

### *Consider the Soul*

We are more than an assortment of chemicals. Science says 60 per cent of our body is but water. Can we imagine ourselves as a water bag with a few chemicals mixed in? Dr Harry Monsen, a professor at the Illinois College of Medicine who analysed the composition of all the chemicals in our body, determined that all the matter of our body is worth about a dollar and nine cents. Is that really how much we're worth?

When a New York construction crane fell on Brigitte Gerney as she was walking along Third Avenue, hundreds of police officers were deputed to reroute the traffic. City officials rushed in with two cranes to lift the crane that fell on her. Bellevue Hospital set up a mobile medical facility on site. Emergency workers worked tirelessly to try and save her. Once she was stabilized, police halted rush hour traffic on the route to the hospital so that she could be immediately transferred there.[13] If we are only worth a little over a dollar, why spend thousands and make such a great effort just to save one person? The fact is that life is invaluable and sacred.

People are prepared to cut off legs, arms or whichever part of the body may be necessary to ensure that life goes on. Still, in the normal course of things, we see people give so much more attention to the body than to the indwelling living soul. This can be likened to maintaining the birdcage while neglecting the bird. To ensure that we are completely nourished, we must prioritize the soul's needs. This means taking time each day to practise spirituality through meditation, to associate with spiritually-minded people, to study sacred texts and to perform acts of service.

When a BMW is involved in a road accident, will the cops try to save the human beings in the car or the costly BMW first? The truth is that we are not bags of water with a few other chemicals mixed in but very powerful and blissful spirit souls residing within these material machines. We are like drivers sitting in our cars. The car has lights,

13 Edward D. Reuss, 'The Fight Against Time', NYCOP, 1999, https://www.nycop.com/Aug_99/The_Fight_Against_Time/body_the_fight_against_time.html

and we have eyes to see. The car has an engine to power its components, and we have a heart to pump our blood. The car has tyres, and we have legs for mobility. Just like the driver of the car, the soul drives this body. Once the soul leaves the body permanently, the body is considered dead.

How do you nourish spirituality?

### *Association*

You are who you associate with. If you want to be spiritual, stay in touch with spiritual people on a regular basis. Out of 168 hours in a week, if you spend at least two hours (less than 2 per cent of the week) associating with spiritually-minded people, it will make a great difference in your life. The iron rod becomes red-hot when heated in the fire and ice-cold when kept in a refrigerator. This association must be based on the principle of inspiration: listening to spiritualists talking about spirituality and taking inspiration from them to apply the principles of spirituality to one's own life. We need to associate with people who are spiritually strong and serious in their spiritual practices, people who intend to make spiritual progress.

### *Spiritual Books*

If you want to become a software engineer, you need to read books related to software engineering suggested by your professors. Similarly, if we want to progress spiritually and uplift our consciousness, we need to read spiritual books suggested by the spiritualists we associate with. It is important to read them on a daily basis. Discussions with spiritually advanced people will help clarify our doubts and thoughts.

### *Simple Lifestyle*

Our presence in this world is very temporary. It is known that, when our time ends, neither will anyone come with us and nor can we take any physical thing with us. Hence, we should utilize our precious human life to cleanse our heart, remove impurities and experience the joy of the soul. For this to happen, we need to adopt a simple lifestyle. Our lifestyle should help support our spiritual aspirations, but should not make us believe 'I am this body or mind'. Simple living leads to stress-free living and soulful thinking. A simple lifestyle involves minimizing our physical needs and thereby maximizing our free time for the cultivation of spiritual practices.

### *Meditation*

The purpose of meditation is to cleanse the heart and control the mind. There are many types of meditation, and information about all of them is available online these days. However, in my life, it is mantra meditation that has been most effective. Although you can meditate at any time of the day, for best results you should cultivate the habit of meditating early in the morning, if possible. Some meditate at noon and others prefer to do it in the evening. Initially, you may find it difficult to focus, as the mind wanders here and there due to its unsteady nature. But there is no need to worry. By adopting a simple lifestyle and with steady practice, you can make progress on the path to a spiritual life.

| Suggestions for Mode of Goodness | Suggestions for Mode of Passion | Suggestions for Mode of Ignorance |
|---|---|---|
| Diet and sleep habits | Give up "I am the doer" mentality | Cut down activities of Q4 |
| Stick to the script | Self-awareness | Cut down on procrastination |
| Yoga, Pranayama and Mantra Meditation | Value-based life | Set a deadline |
| Mantra | Slow down | Develop your spiritual quotient |
| | Improve your listening skills | |
| | Find joy in selfless service | |
| | Develop a sense of humor | |

## 4.2. PRACTISING FORGIVENESS

*To forgive is to set a prisoner free and discover that the prisoner was you.*

—Lewis B. Smedes

When someone hurts us, we tend to develop negative feelings towards them. Whenever we think of the person, feelings of resentment and indignation well up in our heart. This disturbs our inner sanctum and, ultimately, stresses us out. Consider your goal—do you want to achieve inner peace? If so, forgiveness is required. Some offences may be so egregious that forgiveness may feel impossible. But before you deem someone unforgivable, consider the following story.

In 2006, a milk truck driver, Charles Robert, stormed into an Amish school building in Pennsylvania and shot ten girls, killing five. Then, he turned the gun on himself. This tragedy, needless to say, shook the Amish community to the core. But, surprisingly, they did not seek retaliatory measures against any party involved. Instead, they approached the killer's family with empathy and compassion. The father of one of the slain children even forgave the killer on the very day of the atrocity. Many community members even went to the killer's funeral and comforted his widow and three children. They later set up a fund to support his family.[14]

Here are a few more ways to look at forgiveness:

### *Beyond Being Right*

Eastern wisdom declares that our purpose in this world isn't to prove that we are right but to acknowledge where we are wrong and then improve. Often, offering forgiveness can feel like an exhibition of weakness. There is, however, another way of looking at it. We can forgive the person but never forget the wrong they've committed. In this way, we may relinquish our negative feelings while at the same time remaining strong and cautious going forward.

### *Karma*

In my childhood, I once saw something amusing and interesting. A shopkeeper started poking at a cat with a broom to move it so that he could continue to clean the space. The cat, unaware of the person controlling the broom, began attacking the bristles, regarding them as the cause of the

14 West Nickel Mines School shooting, Wikipedia, https://en.wikipedia.org/wiki/West_Nickel_Mines_School_shooting

disturbance. Don't be like the cat. Be aware that the person giving you trouble is actually just an instrument in the hands of your own karma. We can view each situation as an opportunity to learn from our mistakes and curtail the mentality that produces unhelpful reactions.

### *Love*

The nature of the soul is to love and be loved. Money, position and possessions give us power, but the highest power is love. Where there is affection, there is forgiveness. When the child kicks your chest with his tiny legs, you feel happy, thinking, 'His legs are getting strong and soon he will stand and walk.' The point is, there is insufficiency in every relationship—without forgiveness, no relationship can exist in this world.

### *Past Is Past*

Life is a journey and, in that journey, things keep changing. What is very concerning and bothersome to us now may not even be relevant after some time. Hence, we should be cautious about our actions, words and even our thoughts when reacting to something. I remember watching two politicians engage in very serious quarrels thirty years ago. A few years later, both died.

When someone is criticizing you for what you have not done and causing you anxiety, they will share some of your bad karma. This is because they have caused you unnecessary anxiety for the activity you have not done. Hence, we should be careful not to criticize anyone knowingly or unknowingly. When someone is glorifying you and inflating your false ego, they are your enemy. We do incorrect things when we are puffed up with false ego or pride. That every action has an equal and opposite reaction is not only Newton's third law but also nature's. If we forgive, we are forgiven. If we show compassion, we receive compassion. If we show aggression, we receive aggression.

The beautiful real-life story of Sindhutai comes to mind in this connection.

Sindhutai Sapkal[15] was from a poor peasant family in the state of Maharashtra, India. When she wanted to go to school at the age of six, her parents wanted her to take care of their cattle instead. When the cattle were grazing, she would run to school, but her teacher would beat her for being late. When the cattle grazed in the neighbours' fields while she was at school, the neighbours would beat her.

15 About Sindhutai Sapkal (Mai)/Mother of Orphans, Sindhutaisapakal.org, https://www.sindhutaisapakal.org/about-Sindhutail-Sapkal.html

Yet, she considered these times to be happy days. At the age of ten, her childhood ended upon her marriage to a thirty-year-old farmer.

By twenty, she had become the mother of three sons and was pregnant with a fourth child. It was at this point in her life that her travails began. She learnt one day that the local mafia was using local residents, especially women, to work as slaves, and she decided to bring the information to the attention of the local government officials. This angered a mafia member so much that he told her husband obscene, heart-breaking lies about her. He said she was cheating on him with many others, including himself, and that the child in her womb was his own. Sindhutai's husband believed all these lies, became furious, came home and kicked her in the stomach repeatedly until she went unconscious. Assuming that she had died, he dragged her to their barn to make it seem to everyone that she had been trampled to death by an ox. As she lay there, one cow protected her from the other animals by keeping her between its legs. In that position, Sindhutai gave birth to a baby girl. She cut the umbilical cord with a rock. The compassion of the cow saved her life. She embraced the cow and promised to dedicate her life to serving the poor and helpless.

When she went to her parents with her baby for shelter, they rejected her. According to village customs in certain parts of India, the daughter cannot come home after being rejected by her in-laws. She had no one to turn to. Being very young, she was particularly vulnerable. She wound up taking shelter at a cremation ground.

With no hope in sight, Sindhutai contemplated suicide. She decided to end her life by throwing herself and her baby under a train. While walking on the train tracks, she found an old, hungry beggar crying for food. In that cry, she heard God calling on her to help the poor and helpless as she had earlier promised.

But she herself was shattered and hopeless. Her future was wholly uncertain: a baby, no education or skill—what could she do? How could she live in this world? She sat under a tree with her baby to think about her future and observed, after a while, that a branch of the tree was cut and dangling by a thread but still offering her shelter from the blistering heat of the sun. It was then that she found her calling. Despite her dire situation, she decided to take care of homeless orphans.

She immediately started spotting them and getting them off the streets. She sang on railway platforms and begged for money to feed them.

Eventually, some pious people arranged a facility for her as the number of children grew. She became known as the Mother of Orphans. She started providing love, care and education to these children. Over the years, she served as a mother to thousands of children who later became successful doctors, engineers, teachers and professionals.

A few decades later, one old, sickly, homeless derelict came to her orphanage and asked for help. She recognized him. It was her old, cruel husband. He asked for forgiveness, and she not only forgave him but offered him shelter just as she had to countless other downtrodden souls. She accepted him not as a former husband but as her own son. She told her many children of the orphanage to show him love, declaring love to be what he needed the most. As Dr Martin Luther King once said, 'Darkness cannot be removed by darkness, only light can do that; hate cannot be removed by hate but only by love.'

### Forgiveness Exercise

Try and call to mind all the injustices you've suffered. Now imagine a very bright sun in the sky. Picture those injustices being released from your mind like clouds and slowly merging into that burning sun's effulgence. Please repeat the process a few times. Visualizing these impurities leaving the body will empower your mind and heart to actually let go of them.

### 4.3. PRACTISING GRATITUDE

*At times, our own light goes out and is rekindled by a spark from another person. Each of us has cause to think with deep gratitude of those who have lit the flame within us.*

—Albert Schweitzer

*Gratitude is the fairest blossom which springs from the soul.*

—Henry Ward Beecher

*Gratitude turns what we have into enough.*

*Gratitude unlocks the fullness of life. It turns what we have into enough, and more. It turns denial into acceptance, chaos to order, confusion to clarity. It can turn a meal into a feast, a house into a home, a stranger into a friend. Gratitude makes sense of our past, brings peace for today and creates a vision for tomorrow.*

—Melody Beattie

*Gratitude is a powerful catalyst for happiness.*

—Amy Collette

*If I am not grateful, I am a great fool.*

—Anonymous

The word 'gratitude' is derived from the Latin word 'gratus', meaning 'pleasing or thankful'. It is a feeling of appreciation.

### Why Cultivate Gratitude?

We are always being sustained by others. Consider our own mother. She kept us in her womb for nine months and prepared our bodies. She went through so many troubles to finally give birth to us. How many times did she patiently feed us and change our diapers in those early days? Do we remember?

One day, I was in the suburbs of Philadelphia, conducting a workshop. After the workshop, my host Murali, a software engineer, drove me to his place, where I went to sleep in a cosy room. At around 1 p.m., my host's newborn baby started crying so loudly that I could not sleep. My host was a wonderful gentleman. He asked his wife Kalavati to remain in bed and then put the baby on his shoulder and started walking back and forth, trying to lull her back to sleep. Still, the baby continued crying for a long time. At 4 a.m., Kalavati got up and took care of the baby for few more hours, allowing her husband to rest. I sat on my bed and started thinking about my own babyhood and how I had no idea about the problems I must have caused my parents. They must have endured so many sleepless nights because of my crying. My mother must have carried me on her shoulder to put me to sleep like this for many years. I might have wasted a lot of her time while she tried to feed me, to keep me healthy. I might have spoilt many of their plans by falling sick or throwing tantrums. When I realized these things, I became immensely grateful to my mother and father.

I recall another experience I had with a similar family. We were taking a long drive to a spiritual workshop many miles away. When we stopped at a rest area, the wife went to the restroom and handed her husband their baby to hold. Suddenly, the husband told me to hold the baby and went into the restroom himself. Holding the baby for some time, I found my shoulder and arm starting to hurt from the strain. Then I thought of my mother and all the mothers again. For how many years did my mother carry me like this? Her body must also have hurt. Moreover, my mischief as a child probably caused her a great deal of emotional pain. My parents spent a large portion of their lives trying to feed me, take care of my needs, change my diapers, educate me and so on. Their services were endless. When I thought of all these things, I became grateful not only to my mother and father but also to all the parents of the world.

We should be grateful to many people: our parents, their parents (and so on), our relatives, the members of the government who rule our country peacefully to facilitate our growth, the teachers who give us an education and, finally, our divine source, the one that endlessly supplies the essential substances like oxygen, water, food, clothing and shelter and maintains the universe and has fine-tuned it for our journey within it.

When we become grateful, we naturally develop respect for others and, in the process, humility, awakening a service attitude within us. When we develop these wonderful qualities, we start looking at life from a different perspective; instead of thinking of how we can be served by others, we start looking for opportunities to serve. My spiritual teacher and guru, Radhanath Swami, says, 'If we are humble, we can be grateful to even our enemies.' A grateful heart is very forgiving. Also, a grateful heart is one that wants to serve with eagerness, with care, with compassion. To lead a peaceful life, one should be prideless and grateful.

Consider the following story about the true power of gratitude. Dhruva was the son of King Uttanapada and Queen Suniti. He had a stepbrother born of his father and stepmother Suruchi, whom King Uttanapada favoured among his queens. One day, when Dhruva saw his stepbrother sitting on the lap of his father, he too felt the desire to sit on his father's lap. However, when he tried to climb up, his stepmother told him not to, saying he had to die and take birth from *her* womb to gain the right to be on the throne. Hurt by the scornful words of his stepmother, young Dhruva, profusely crying, went to his mother for solace. His mother told him not to wish inauspiciousness to anyone as we suffer the same pain that we inflict on others. She consoled him saying that people obtain things in this world by the mercy of God and if he wanted to become the heir to the throne, he had to try and receive God's mercy, for God could make even the impossible possible. She informed him that sages often went into the forest to perform austerities and meditation with the aim of attaining God's grace.

Inspired, Dhruva left in the middle of the night for the forest to seek the grace of God. The great sage

Narada appeared soon thereafter and gave him a mantra to meditate upon. With Narada's blessings and his own intense austerity, Dhruva managed to get God to appear before him and confer many blessings upon him, including rulership of the kingdom, as he desired. After ruling the planet for a long time, when it was time for him to return to the spiritual world, messengers appeared to escort him into a celestial airplane that would take him there. At that moment, Dhruva thought of his mother with gratitude. On account of her instructions, he had attained everything. He did not want to return to the spiritual world without her. The divine messengers revealed to him then that his mother was already on her way to the spiritual world as well. Dhruva was exceedingly grateful to all those who had helped him attain material and spiritual success.[16]

My guru says, 'Gratitude is not just saying "thank you". Real gratitude goes very deep. It means to reciprocate. If someone saves you when you are in trouble, real gratitude is not walking by and saying thank you. Real gratitude means to reciprocate with an attitude of service.' Dhruva showed this by his refusing to return to the spiritual

16 Srimad Bhagavat Purana

realm without his dear mother, who had been the cause of his ascent.

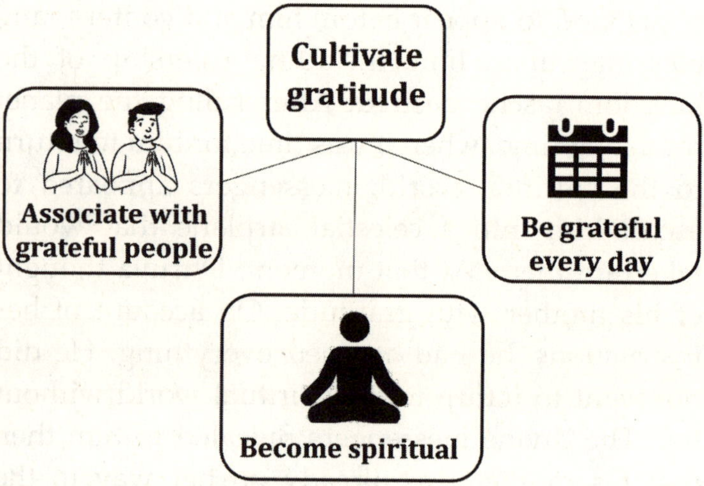


## How to Cultivate Gratitude

### *Be Grateful Everyday*

Consider the following statistics, which may help you think of how lucky you are. On a daily basis, 690 million people go to bed hungry. One billion six hundred million people do not have a home to sleep in. Ninety-five per cent of the world's population have health problems. Only 6.7 per cent of the people in the world have a Bachelor's degree. According to a national survey conducted in 2019 by the insurance company Cigna, 61 per cent of Americans consider themselves lonely. If you have a steady income and are living with your family members in a cosy dwelling, you are extremely fortunate. Do we consider these simple things blessings? Are we grateful for all the rare gifts we have been given? It is a very good practice to maintain a list of items for which we are grateful. We should be thankful to God for continuously providing us all these wonderful gifts.

### *Associate with Grateful People*

People who are grateful are usually humble. A humble heart is a grateful heart. Humble people and spiritual people find ways and means to be grateful even in difficult situations. By regularly hanging out with grateful people, learning from them and listening to their experiences, we slowly imbibe gratitude. The key point of such associations, as mentioned before, is inspiration. If we are inspired by people, then we enjoy hanging out with them and doing things together. We learn from them and help them. When we do this regularly, even without our knowledge, our heart becomes filled with an attitude of gratitude.

### *Become Spiritual*

What is the goal of this universe? Why are there different seasons? Why should the human body endure the difficulties of birth, old age, disease and death? Science explains the functioning of the universe but has never revealed its goal. The ancient wisdom texts explain that this universe is a place of reformation, created to give spirit souls opportunities to cleanse their impurities, namely lust, anger, greed, illusion, pride and envy. Hence, the goal of life is to cleanse the impurities of the heart so that we can go back to our original home: the spiritual world. Our presence in this body and in this world is temporary. If we understand this fact, we can then try to make a difference in our life and in the lives of others by sharing spiritual knowledge. This is a world of duality. Nothing is permanent in it, neither happiness nor distress. The only constant is change. Life is but a journey towards the realization of our true self. When we are clear about our goal, we accept every situation with gratitude, whether it is characterized by happiness or distress, and treat it as an opportunity for the upliftment of our soul. A grateful person is an unstressed person. Spirituality is practised in association with grateful people. Serious spiritualists with a firm footing in knowledge are always grateful. By being associated with them, we become grateful and thus keep stress at bay.

### 4.4. PRACTISING A SERVICE ATTITUDE

The inherent nature of the soul is to love and be loved. This love is manifested through service. Everyone in this world serves someone. Parents serve their children, employees serve their bosses and even those with no kids or job likely have a pet animal that they are sure to feed and clean up after. But in all these examples, something is expected in return; hence, some dissatisfaction may ensue. Selfless service, on the other hand, is what the soul truly craves. Because such selfless service is wholly in line with our nature, we automatically feel satisfied upon engaging in it. This may take the form of serving the poor, our community, society at large or even the planet. In any environment, if we serve with abandon, stress will give way to satisfaction.

If you think about it, most of our problems originate in the mind, that is, in the way we perceive a certain thing or situation. By stepping out of the 'I and my' zone and into the realm of selfless service, we gain a new perspective on life. Instead of becoming absorbed in our own comfort and enjoyment, we focus on that of others. In this state of mind, we start to understand just how insignificant some of our issues are and instead find pleasure in helping others. This is what Saint Francis meant when he said, 'For it is in giving that we receive.' While it may appear that we are giving so much time and energy to someone else, in reality we receive the most important gift in return: tranquillity and peace of mind.

The happiest people in the world are not necessarily the ones who have taken the most from others, but those who live to give. While takers live in constant anxiety about maintaining their assets and position, givers are always busy thinking about the welfare of others. One example in this regard is India's Kalyana Sundaram. During his thirty-five-year career as a librarian, he donated each month's paycheck to charities that looked after the welfare of those less fortunate. He would work a few odd jobs on the side to address his own needs. After retiring, he donated his entire retirement fund to similar organizations. This man had a taste for giving; he realized just how liberating it is to give up gluttony and make giving one's main joy in life. While we may not be able to imitate his level of selfless service, we can at least recognize the standard he exemplified and know in our hearts that selflessness is more nourishing than selfishness.[17]

Another example of this powerful mentality is James Cash Penney. J.C. Penney started his career with a salary of $25 per month but eventually rose to build a chain of wildly successful department stores. By the time he departed from this world in 1971, he had 1,660 stores with an overall annual revenue of $4 billion. However, he understood the ephemeral nature of this world. He knew that positions and possessions in this world are very temporary. When he realized that everyone had to go one day and carry with them nothing but their pious deeds, he became a philanthropist and made unprecedented donations to the Young Men's Christian Association (YMCA), Boy Scouts, National 4-H club, Allied Youth Inc. and many other noble non-profits.[18]

---

17 'The Man of the Millennium Palam Kalyanasundaram Spreads Kindness Like a Bonfire', ViralIndianDiary.com, 13 February 2022, https://www.viralindiandiary.com/the-man-of-the-millennium-palam-kalyanasundaram/

18 Community, Yankton Daily, https://www.yankton.net/community/; Afterschool alliance, www.afterschoolalliance.org

A final example of the power of a service attitude is King Rantidev.[19] The Bhagavata Purana describes him as a king who treated everyone with respect. He saw the spirit soul present in every species and served each one with love and affection. He was known for his charity and philanthropy. One time, after a forty-eight-day fast, just as he was about to eat, a pious and hungry man came to his doorstep asking for food. The king duly gave a portion of his food to the hungry man and satisfied him. Then, as the king was about to start eating, another man came asking for food. Rantidev gave him another portion of his own food and satisfied him. Shortly afterwards, yet another man came with his dogs, asking of the king food for him and his dogs. Rantidev gave away the rest of the food he had and satisfied the man and his dogs. Only water remained.

Because he had been fasting for so long, he knew that if he didn't at least drink some water, his very life could be in jeopardy. But, of course, just as he was about to drink, another man came running into the palace, asking Rantidev to quench his thirst. Rantidev then had to choose between his life and that of his guest. He chose

19 Srimad Bhagavata Purana, 9th canto.

to save the life of his guest. What he said as his body shivered from malnourishment is worth noting: 'I do not want mystic perfections, I do not want salvation from suffering and the cycle of birth and death. All I want is to stay with these ordinary living entities and try to relieve their suffering.' Having said this, he gave his portion of water to the needy man.

## The Benefits of Serving

### *Stress and Depression Reduction*

The joy of the Christmas season comes from giving! Now imagine that feeling lasting all year. Well, it can! By staying in the mode of giving, you can sustain a sense of joy, a sense of purpose and,

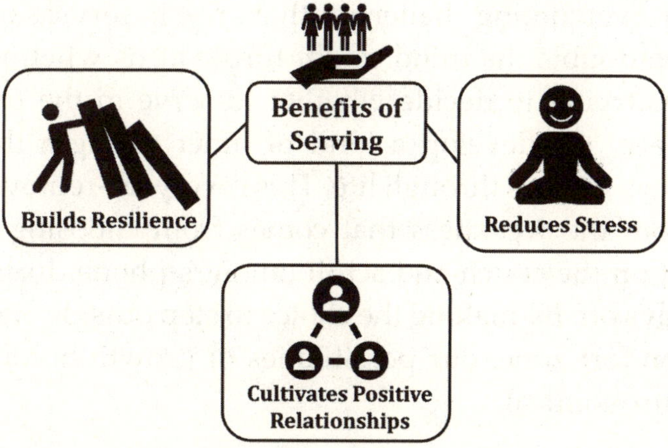

as a result, a stress-free sense of satisfaction. Such a healthy state of mind naturally wards off feelings of anxiety and depression. In fact, in a study conducted by the London School of Economics, it was found that the more people volunteered, the happier they felt.

### *Positive Relationships*

By situating ourselves in communities that believe in service, we can naturally find high-quality individuals. Serving together forges relationships with such people that help solidify the theme of service in our lives. In this age of self-centredness, unity amongst selfless souls is a great asset.

### *Resilience*

By overcoming challenges that arise in service and the doubts the mind might throw at us when we are trying to decide whether to serve in the first place, we develop a kind of inner strength that stays with us through life. This is very far-removed from the weakness that comes from choosing to sit on the couch and scroll on one's phone during days off. By making the choice to step outside one's comfort zone, our possibilities of growth become astronomical.

## 4.5. RELAXATION, MEDITATION, SONIC (MANTRA) MEDITATION, AND PRAYER

### Relaxation

Now we will reiterate a few of the techniques previously mentioned for instilling peace in the mind. The good thing about these techniques is that they not only calm one down in the middle of a stressful experience but also serve as preventative treatments that guard against future freak-outs.

### Progressive Muscle Relaxation (PMR)

Anger tenses our muscles. If we relax our muscles, our mind follows suit. PMR is most effectively performed under the guidance of a teacher, but there are many great videos online that can walk you through it. You will be instructed to tense the muscles in your neck as you breathe in for five to ten seconds and then relax them completely as you fully exhale. As you tense your muscles, picture your life force flowing into the muscles to strengthen them. As you relax, let all of your anger exit your body. By practising this technique on a daily basis, we can become less susceptible to anger.

## Acupuncture

Acupuncture is an ancient Chinese medical practice meant to relieve pressure and energy blockages in the body. While it is primarily used to manage pain, it can also be employed to manage an ailing mind. Try acupuncture for an easy way to quickly feel a lot more relaxed.

## Aromatherapy

Essential oils and plant extracts are used in aromatherapy to help improve both mental and physical health. Aromatherapy acts either through the sense of smell or through the application of essential oils on the body. Research has shown that aromatherapy can alter the way the brain perceives things and thus calm the mind amidst stressful conditions.

## Hydrotherapy

Taking a dip in cool water triggers endorphins in the body, which gives us a feeling of physical relaxation and mental tranquillity. Try regularly taking dips in natural bodies of water. This will naturally improve your mental health.

### Tai Chi

Tai chi is another practice developed in China that has been proven to greatly reduce stress and anxiety. It is a combination of exercise and meditation. Through graceful, flowing movements and deep breathing, the practitioner finds a deep sense of peace and overall well-being. The regular practice of tai chi helps assure peace of mind.

### Massage

The body and mind are integrally connected; if one is disturbed, the other almost always follows suit. Thus, sometimes even a physical treatment can have very powerful but subtle mental results. The massage is one such treatment—relaxing the muscles and working out the knots in the body can also relieve the knots in the mind.

### Meditation

While the mind to a large extent remains a mystery to modern science, the ancient wisdom texts offer volumes of literature describing not just the mind but also how to control it. The main process recommended for controlling the mind is meditation, which has now become a buzzword due to its ability to keep one calm and focused.

Some practise it for psychological benefits, others for spiritual benefits and still others for overall wellness. But the key aspect of meditation, regardless of one's aim, is to bring the mind to focus on a single point, to bring the mind back to that point no matter where it wanders. Let's take a look at a few different kinds of meditation. Which one suits you best?

### *Zen Meditation*

Zen is a Buddhist meditation technique. Once comfortably seated with your back erect, focus on your breath. As your breathing normalizes, simply observe it. When distractions arise, you must simply bring your mind back to your breath until your mind becomes still.

### *Mindfulness Meditation*

A healthy mind is fully conscious of its surroundings, thoughts and feelings without being overly reactive. Mindfulness meditation is a process by which one gains complete awareness of the present moment. It is similar to zen meditation in that, after streamlining one's breath through uniform inhalations and exhalations, one becomes conscious of it and, when distractions arise, one re-routes the mind to the breath.

### *Transcendental Meditation (TM)*

Even though it uses a mantra, TM is a silent meditation technique in which one focuses the mind on the syllables of the mantra within one's mind. Once one receives the mantra from a TM teacher, one sits and focuses on it for fifteen to twenty minutes daily.

### *Vipassana Meditation*

Vipassana is another Buddhist meditation practice. The practitioner is meant to observe the flow of thoughts coming into and going out of the mind. The idea is to be an objective witness to the thoughts while not reacting to any of them in a negative or positive way. One also controls one's breathing in a way that helps the mind objectively witness its own activities.

### *Kundalini Yoga Meditation*

Our body has seven chakras or discs of energy, connected to different nerves along the spine. Kundalini is meant to awaken the energy dormant in the root chakra at the base of the spine and spread it to revitalize and replenish the body and mind. The practitioner chants a mantra and practises a specific breathing process. This is perhaps the most complicated of all the practices mentioned and so an expert guide is recommended.

### *Loving Kindness Meditation*

Practitioners of loving kindness meditation generate feelings of love, affection, kindness and compassion for themselves and others. These feelings can be targeted at anyone. It is especially recommended that one direct them towards those one has relational problems with.

### *Dhyana Yoga Meditation*

This is also called ashtanga yoga meditation or the eight-step meditation process. The eight steps are: yama (moral obligations), niyama (moral restraints), asana (yoga postures), pranayama (breath control), pratyahara (withdrawal of senses), dharana (focus), dhyana (meditation) and samadhi (complete absorption). After bringing the body to a balance by following the above initial steps, one meditates on the aspect of God within the heart.

### *Sonic (Mantra) Meditation*

Unlike other organs of our body, the mind is very subtle. We can perceive it through the thoughts it generates. Hence, we need a tool/process that can reach into the mind and rectify its functioning. Mantra meditation stands above other tools in this regard, in that it gives the mind an explicit, positive, spiritual sound to dwell on. As mentioned previously, mantra vibrations deliver us from the agitations of our mind. A mantra, then, is a kind of sonic therapy that delivers the mind from all lower encumbrances.

### *Effects of Meditation on Brainwaves*

When we relax, our brain generates alpha waves. Alpha waves deepen our sense of relaxation and provide feelings of peace and pleasure. When a meditator sits in a comfortable position with closed eyes and begins chanting mantras, their brain gradually shifts to producing alpha waves, giving them a sense of peace that stays with them throughout the day. It is important to note that, in this state, we are still fully conscious and self-aware. We can consciously choose to infuse our mind with positive qualities like determination, patience, enthusiasm and peace. Set a positive tone for each day with a powerful meditative experience each morning.

### *Benefits of Sonic Meditation*

A study on Hare Krishna mantra meditation suggests that mantra meditation plays a vital role in the formation of a healthy lifestyle and it helps in the prevention of chronic diseases.[20] Twenty years ago, a study published in the British Medical Journal compared the effects of reciting either the mantra 'Om mani padme ham' or the Ave Maria (Hail Mary in Latin) on respiratory and cardiovascular rhythms.[21] Reciting either of these slowed respiration to six breaths per minute. Electrocardiogram, blood pressure and brain circulation measurements of the people chanting the mantra and reciting the Ave Maria looked the same. These outputs were very different from those associated with spontaneous breathing. The authors concluded that mantras may have beneficial effects on cardiovascular rhythms simply because they slow down breathing.

20 https://pubmed.ncbi.nlm.nih.gov/31043916

21 Bernardi, L., Sleight, P., Bandinelli, G., Cencetti, S., Fattorini, L., Wdowczyc-Szulc, J., Lagi, A. (2001). Effect of rosary prayer and yoga mantras on autonomic cardiovascular rhythms: comparative study. *BMJ*, 323(7327), 1446–49.

Another study undertaken at Duke University found that four weeks of practising mantra meditation on a daily basis resulted in significantly decreased levels of stress and anxiety.[22] One study focused on the levels of mental tranquillity achieved while chanting the Hare Krishna maha-mantra ('Hare Krishna Hare Krishna Krishna Krishna Hare Hare/ Hare Rama Hare Rama Rama Rama Hare Hare') on the one hand and, on the other, a made-up mantra composed of meaningless Sanskrit syllables. Those who chanted 'Hare Krishna', the maha-mantra, were found to have drastically lower levels of stress and anxiety than those who chanted the placebo mantra.[23] The mantra has also been scientifically proven to relieve PTSD in

---

22 Lane, J. D., Seskevich, J. E., per cent Pieper, C. F. (2007). Brief meditation training can improve perceived stress and negative mood. *Alternative Therapies in Health and Medicine*, 13(1), 38–44.

23 Wolf, D. B., per cent Abell, N. (2003). Examining the effects of meditation techniques on psychosocial functioning. Research on Social Work Practice, 13(1), 27–42.[6]. Wolf, D. B. (1999). A psychometric analysis of the three gunas. *Pyschological Reports*, 84, 1379–90.

veterans[24] and has even been found to get rid of joint pain![25]

Another study found that kirtan kriya (rhythmic chanting of mantras accompanied by musical instruments) affected gene expression. The practice of kirtan kriya by family members/ caregivers of dementia patients was found to result in the decreased activity of factors that control proinflammatory gene expression and increased activity of factors that control gene expression related to antiviral function,[26] suggesting that this mantra-based meditation helps achieve healthier immune function. To assess its effects on cognitive function in individuals with subjective cognitive

---

24 Bormann, J. E., Thorp, S. R., Wetherell, J. L., Golshan, S., per cent Jang, A. (2013). Meditation based mantram intervention for veterans with posttraumatic stress disorder: A randomized trial. *Psychological Trauma*, 213(5), 259–67.

25 Monk-Turner, E. (2003). 'The benefits of meditation: experimental findings'. *The Social Science Journal*, 40, pp. 465–70.

26 Black, D. S., Cole, S. W., Irwin, M. R., Breen, E., St Cyr, N. M., Nazarian, N., ... Lavresky, H. (2013). Yogic meditation reverses NF-KB and IRF-related transcriptome dynamics in leukocytes of family dementia caregivers in a randomized controlled trial. *Psychoneuroendocrinology*, 38(3), 348–55.

decline, kirtan kriya was compared to a standard memory-enhancement training programme. Significant improvement in memory was seen with both interventions, but only kirtan kriya resulted in significant improvement in executive function (mental processes that control behaviour).[27] Therefore, mantra-based meditation might be at least as effective as standard treatments for cognitive decline.

### *Prayer*

Prayer is another proven way of reducing stress and accessing tranquillity. It has been shown that regular prayer can even change the brain's chemistry for the better. Specifically, it has been seen that people who regularly engage in meditation and prayer increase the size of their frontal lobe, which is responsible for concentration and focus.[28] Besides the physical effects, prayer also helps relieve much of the pressure that accumulates on one's shoulders as stressful situations pile up.

---

27 Eyre, H. A., Siddarth, P., Acevedo, B., Van, D. K., Paholpak, P., Ercoli, L. Lavretsky, H. (2017). A randomized controlled trial of Kundalini yoga in mild cognitive impairment. International Psychogeriatrics, 29(4), 557–567.

28 Kluger, J. The Biology of Belief, Time Magazine. (2009)

Having to bear it all oneself is daunting; on the other hand, it is comforting to know that a higher power is right there with us to help show us the way if we so desire.

So, what should we pray for? In this connection, there is a relevant story in the Bhagavat Purana about the plight of Gajendra, the king of the elephants. Gajendra was extremely powerful and was always accompanied by his many wives. Once, while bathing in a beautiful lake, he was attacked by a vicious crocodile. His wives tried to save him, but, perceiving the situation to be hopeless, they fled. Then he became aware of the fact that we come alone into this world and also leave alone from here. Realizing that there was no one left to save him besides God, Gajendra, in great desperation and humility, cried out, 'My Lord! You are the supremely merciful controller of all! Please deliver me both from this distress and from my entanglement in the material world!' The Lord responded by appearing and carrying Gajendra away from the crocodile and into the spiritual world.[29]

On the other side of the spectrum is the story of Queen Kunti, who prayed for calamities to continue occurring in her life, as each one inspired

29 Srimad Bhagavata Purana, 8th canto.

in her greater conviction about taking shelter in the Lord. She hoped not for a comfortable life but for the discomfort of her sojourn to inspire her to leave all material attachments behind. Whether we pray for a better material situation or a more challenging one, the act of turning towards a higher power will yield immense benefits.

***Four Steps for Powerful Prayers:***

1. Glorify God and His beauty, love and compassion.
2. With a humble heart, admit your faults and impurities. You may also express your gratitude for the various gifts that you've received. It is important to note that, without humility and gratitude, prayers are not as effective.
3. Ask for a blessing. What blessing should we ask for? We can pray for relief from suffering, to recover from an ailment or for prosperity, but it is best to ask for those things which will not be taken from us in time. Things like beauty, health and status will always come and go but inner strength, discerning nature and a pure and loving heart can remain forever.

4. The last step is to seek forgiveness for the things we've done in the past. We should correspondingly pray for the strength to rise above such weaknesses and bad habits.

The essential goal of prayer is to establish a connection with God and seek His grace with a loving mood of gratitude towards Him and his subjects. When the heart is filled with gratitude and love, what room is there for stress and depression?

## SUMMARY

### Managing Stress at the Levels of Body and Mind

**Body:** Regulate your diet and sleep cycle and refrain from activities that will harm you physically.

**Mind:** It magnifies problems and makes us weak. It imagines problems to be bigger than they are. It creates and spreads negativity. It denies opportunities for service and growth.

### How to regulate the mind?

1. Look on the bright side
2. Be aware of the world's temporary nature
3. Live for yourself
4. Sense Control
5. Simplicity

## Personality Types

***Stress Management Suggestions for Those in the Mode of Goodness***

1. Dietary and Sleeping Habits
2. Stick to the Script
3. Yoga, Pranayama and Mantra Meditation

***Stress Management Suggestions for People in the Mode of Passion***

1. Give up the 'I am the doer' mentality
2. Develop self-awareness
3. Develop a value-based life
4. Slow down
5. Find joy in selfless service
6. Develop a sense of humour

***Stress Management Suggestions for People in the Mode of Ignorance***

1. Cut out the not-important, not-urgent activities
2. Set and adhere to deadlines
3. Nourish your spirituality by associating with spiritual people and adopting a life of regulation and meditation

4. Consider the soul

### Practising Forgiveness

#### *Steps to Forgive Someone Who Has Hurt You*

1. Recognize the problem: you're harbouring negative feelings
2. Repent for desiring bad things to happen to them
3. Resist negative feelings

### A Few Points on Forgiveness

1. Without forgiveness, relationships cannot exist
2. Life is a journey in which we must keep moving forward
3. Transcend the need to be right
4. When we forgive, we are also forgiven

### How to Cultivate Gratitude?

1. Make expressing gratitude a habit
2. Associate with grateful people
3. Become spiritual

### Six Major Benefits of a Service Attitude

1. Reduces stress and depression
2. Inspires positive relationships
3. Subdues negative thoughts
4. Produces joy and happiness
5. Builds resilience

### Relaxation, Meditation, Sonic (Mantra) Meditation, Prayer

#### *Relaxation Techniques*

Relaxation methods are various methods of handling and managing stress:

1. Progressive muscle relaxation
2. Acupuncture
3. Aromatherapy
4. Hydrotherapy
5. Tai chi
6. Massage
7. Meditation
8. Prayer

## Meditation

Meditation is a proven way of reducing stress and anxiety. There are several different types of meditation:

1. Zen meditation
2. Mindfulness meditation
3. Transcendental meditation
4. Vipassana meditation
5. Kundalini yoga meditation
6. Loving kindness meditation
7. Dhyana yoga meditation
8. Sonic meditation

## Benefits of Sonic Meditation

1. Inspires a positive lifestyle
2. Helps prevent chronic diseases
3. Improves cardiovascular rhythm
4. Significantly reduces stress and anxiety
5. Augments the mode of goodness
6. Improves sleep
7. Relieves joint pain
8. Improves cognition and memory

## Prayer

Prayer is a key to progress in life. It is a way of communicating with God.

### *Benefits of Prayer*

1. Creates an aura of positivity
2. Helps reduce anxiety, sadness and blood pressure
3. Improves sleep, digestion and breathing
4. Inspires positive thinking

**QUESTIONS**

1. How can you tune your body to better handle stress?

____________________________________________

____________________________________________

____________________________________________

____________________________________________

2. How can you tune your mind to better handle stress?

3. What steps will you take to cultivate the mode of goodness?

4. What are the steps of forgiveness?

5. Have you ever felt any different after completely forgiving someone?

6. How have you expressed gratitude in the past?

7. How do we cultivate gratitude?

8. Name one selfless service that you render regularly. For whom do you do it and why?

9. From your experience, can you list the benefits of a service attitude?

_______________

_______________

_______________

_______________

10. Do you employ a specific method of relaxation? If yes:

    a. What is your method of relaxation?

    _______________

    b. How long have you been using it?

    _______________

    c. How many times do you employ it weekly?

    _______________

    d. How long does the method take to perform?

    _______________

    e. What is your experience of using it?

    _______________

f. How will you improve the process for better results?

______________________________________________

11. Do you regularly perform any type of meditation? If yes:

a. How many times do you meditate each week?

______________________________________________

b. How much time do you spend in meditation?

______________________________________________

c. What is your process of meditation?

______________________________________________

d. How long have you been practising meditation?

______________________________________________

e. What have the results been so far?

______________________________________________

f. How will you improve your meditation skills?

___

12. Do you regularly pray? If yes:

a. How many times a week do you pray?

___

b. How much time do you devote to a given prayer?

___

c. What is the objective/goal of your prayers?

___

d. How long have you been praying for?

___

e. What do you do to help you focus during prayer?

___

f. How will you improve your focus?

___

# A Note on Sources

All references to religious writings, stories and myths have been taken from the Ramayana, Mahabharata, Bhagavada Gita and Bhagavata Purana, which have been accessed by me in the original Sanskrit. The translation from Sanskrit is my own.

The several quotations in the book have been taken from https://www.goodreads.com/ and https://www.brainyquote.com/.

**Yugal Kishore Das**

# Acknowledgements

I am immensely grateful to my beloved Guru Radhanath Swami, who is the guiding light in my life.

I am grateful to Shyamananda Das from Chowpatty Temple for his support and guidance. I sincerely thank Gauranga Das for his wisdom and inputs on *Anger Management*; Radheshyam Das for his inputs on *Stress Management*; Chaitanya Caran for his suggestions and comments, especially with the book titles.

I sincerely thank Harsha Vardhan Chitta for his encouragement, without which this series would not have come into existence. He has been pushing me to write for the past ten years. He constantly supported this project by providing many much-needed resources. I am grateful to him and his wife Manasa for their warmth and affection.

I am immensely thankful to Prof. Ramana Vinjamuri for his inputs and guidance. He invested his precious time, energy and talent in all the phases of the project. He was involved at every step and in all the important decisions. He drew all the illustrations used in the books and also conceived and designed all the covers. I am deeply grateful to him and his wife Deepti for their continued support in my life. I sincerely thank Dr Shrawan Chittor Surender for his inputs and guidance on this project. I am very grateful to him and his wife Shilpa Surender for their constant support.

I am also grateful to Anupama Das for editing this book. He also many valuable suggestions to make the content appealing.

My sincere thanks goes out to the following: Dr Atul Kapoor, MD (Physician), and Dr Anisha Kapoor, MD (Physician), for their medical advice on *Stress Management*; Dr Kavitha Vasu, MD (Psychiatry), for her time and valuable suggestions on all three books; Dr Alka Desai, MD (Psychiatry), for her inputs on *Anger Management* and *Stress Management*; Dr Padmaja Vuppala, MD (Psychiatry), and her daughter Anusha; Dr Padma Morisetty, MD (Physician), and Dr Uma Pittala, MD (Physician); Dr Dan Fink MD (Physician); Dr Adria Savino, MD (Psychiatry).

I sincerely thank Dr Raman Chopra and his wife Dr Vanita Chopra for their support and encouragement.

I am grateful to my father (late) Satyanarayana Murthy Poolla for his love and affection mother Saraswathi, brother Veerraju, sister Rajyalakshmi for their affection and support throughout my life.

Thanks are also due to Nanda Niketan, Shyam Kishore, Bhagavat Acharya, Sundarhari, Shyamananda Krishna, Ravi Morisetty and Ram Tulasi for their support.

I extend my thanks to HarperCollins for publishing this book. I am grateful to Rakesh Chander and Hina Khajuria and their team, as well as our literary agent Dipti Patel to have made this project a pleasant reality.

And, finally, thanks to all of you readers who accepted the contents of these books with a graceful heart.

# About the Author

Yugal Kishore Das is a globally renowned speaker, monk, lifestyle mentor, and coach. He holds a masters degree in mathematics, and bachelors degrees in science and law from various Indian universities. He has also studied software programming.

He is based in Michigan, but has travelled all over the US, imparting spiritual insights on work–life balance, relationships and mindfulness. He has also travelled widely to East Asia, the

Middle East and Europe, conducting seminars on personality development and providing guidance to students, professionals and corporate leaders. He has conducted seminars at universities such as Carnegie Mellon, University of Pittsburgh, University of Cincinnati, Wayne State University and Lawrence Tech University. He has also held seminars for multinational corporations like Procter & Gamble and Ford Motor Company, among others.

His goal is to build like-minded communities and equip them with the tools to address the problems of the modern world and toxic work culture. He believes that people can live in peace and harmony with nature if they have the right tools and support.

Please visit www.yugalkishore.com for more information, and to reach out to the author, please mail at contact@yugalkishore.com.

# HarperCollins *Publishers* India

At HarperCollins India, we believe in telling the best stories and finding the widest readership for our books in every format possible. We started publishing in 1992; a great deal has changed since then, but what has remained constant is the passion with which our authors write their books, the love with which readers receive them, and the sheer joy and excitement that we as publishers feel in being a part of the publishing process.

Over the years, we've had the pleasure of publishing some of the finest writing from the subcontinent and around the world, including several award-winning titles and some of the biggest bestsellers in India's publishing history. But nothing has meant more to us than the fact that millions of people have read the books we published, and that somewhere, a book of ours might have made a difference.

As we look to the future, we go back to that one word—a word which has been a driving force for us all these years.

Read.

Harper Collins

HARPER PERENNIAL

HARPER BUSINESS

HARPER BLACK

हार्पर हिन्दी

HarperCollins *Children's Books*

HARPER DESIGN

HARPER VANTAGE

Harper Sport